CREATING A HOME

MAKING STYLISH SOFT FURNISHINGS

WARD LOCK

CONTENTS

© Ward Lock Limited, 1993
A Cassell Imprint
Villiers House, 41-47 Strand, London WC2N 5JE

Based on *Creating A Home*
First Edition © Eaglemoss Publications Limited, 1986

ISBN 0 7063 7208 5

Printed in Spain by Cayfosa Industria Grafica

INTRODUCTION

Far from being a neglected afterthought to a decorating scheme, soft furnishings should be at the forefront of interior design. Designing and making soft furnishings are among the most exciting and rewarding aspects of home decoration.

Another volume in the 'Creating a Home' series – **Curtains and soft furnishings** – gave detailed instructions for making basic window coverings, cushions and accessories. **Making stylish soft furnishings** goes a step further to inspire you to create more unusual interiors and suggest a myriad of ways to enhance the style and atmosphere of your home.

Starting with windows, this book helps you make the most of a room's most important and natural focal points. With so many ways to dress a window, the reference section on different styles will prove invaluable, whether your preference is for straightforward curtains or lavish drapes, plain or valanced headings, tailored blinds or fancy festoons. There's advice on dealing with a range of shapes from modern casements to Georgian bays, even an unusual arched window. And, when it comes to choosing the all-important 'designer' touches – tiebacks, pelmets and valances, swags and tails – you'll find plenty of advice to help you produce a really stylish effect.

One way to enliven a room scheme is with unusual decorative effects on the walls - learn how to cover walls with fabric, try out a special paint finish, or even design your own mural.

A special haven of retreat, the bedroom comes in for special attention with ideas for creating beautifully dressed beds, customised to match your decor. Whether you simply want to make your own bedlinen or try your hand at more elaborate drapes and canopies, the instructions in this section are straightforward to follow.

Making stylish soft furnishings also contains a comprehensive guide to upholstery fabrics, complete with photographs and detailed descriptions. There are also step-by-step instructions for making loose covers for rounded furniture, re-upholstering drop-in seats and re-caning worn-out chairs.

Whether you are completely re-decorating or just giving your home a fresh look, this book is sure to fire your imagination.

WINDOW TREATMENTS

The windows in your home can be dressy focal points or simple backdrops.

As the source of daylight, windows are natural focal points. Unfortunately, they also let in noise, dirt and cold air. Window dressing can be practical in terms of regulating noise and light; done with skill, it is also an important element of the style and atmosphere of a room.

The windows in your home tend to differ in size from room to room. As a result, your choice of window treatment has a similarly varying influence on how the room looks. In addition, some rooms contain more upholstered (and often patterned) furniture than others with which the window dressing must blend.

When deciding on window treat-ments, a few general guidelines will help to point you in the right direction. After that, personal taste must take over. Windows always look best if they are in keeping with the style of the room – heavy curtains with a deep pelmet or swags and tails for formal rooms; straight-forward roller blinds for a casual style, frilled austrian blinds for a dressy, feminine room.

Do you want to make a feature of the window area – or play it down? Do the proportions of the window need to be disguised? How much privacy is needed – and is there a need to filter light during the daytime?

Floral style
Dressy swags and tails make an elegant feature of the window; this style of curtain cuts out a certain amount of daylight, even when tied back.

△ A splash of colour
In a bright colour, venetian blinds create a streamlined, bold window covering. When the slats are tilted to allow more light into the room, the colour becomes less dominant.

The turquoise glow which the blinds throw on to the glass-topped coffee table is echoed in the work table and the turquoise flecks in the cushion covers.

▷ An angular pelmet
Pelmets can be made in almost any shape imaginable. Here a pelmet with modern, zigzag edge adds dramatic visual appeal to curtains, but without making them fussy. Tiebacks soften the line of the curtains. Roman blinds in a sheer fabric with just a hint of pattern shade the window during the daytime.

The curtain fabric echoes the colour of the cushions, while that of the roman blinds reflects the primrose legs of the coffee table.

DRESSING UP THE WINDOW

Some window coverings — swags and tails or austrian blinds, for example — are by definition dressy. Others can be elaborate or informal, depending on their shape, and the type, colour and pattern of the fabric which is used.

Curtains are perhaps the most flexible of all window coverings. Headings range from simple gathers to complicated arrangements of pleats. A rich pattern or bright colour makes an eye-catching feature in any room. Curtains which match or contrast with upholstery fabrics can add the finishing touch to a co-ordinated colour scheme.

Whatever fabric you select, don't skimp on both quantity *and* quality. If necessary, purchase more of a cheaper fabric so as to create generous curtains which fall in rich folds.

The finishing touches — pelmets, curtain rods, tiebacks and so on — can turn a simple curtain into an impressive feature. Top straight curtains with a deeply frilled valance, hang them from a brass curtain rod, add tiebacks, trim them with tassels or edge them with a contrasting fabric.

Blinds The fabric you choose can dramatize the clean lines of roller or vertical louvre blinds. The pleats and gathers in austrian and roman blinds themselves draw the eye. Venetian blinds can be striped — perhaps to match the colours of the soft furnishings — for a bold look.

△ **Understated elegance**
Simplicity of line, together with creative detailing, turn otherwise plain curtains into a masterpiece of window dressing.

The curtains are hung from a simple wooden rod fixed by elaborate brackets. An edging of darker toning blue adds definition and accentuates the flowing line of the sloping over-curtain.

▷ **A wall of colour**
Vibrant red vertical louvre blinds form a simple but striking covering for patio doors, and can easily be drawn back to allow access to the patio.

Like venetian blinds, the slats can swivel through 180° to control precisely the amount of light entering. The blinds can stack to the right or the left or, as here, they can part in the middle like curtains.

△ **Striped co-ordination**
A relatively small and
uninteresting window is
often best treated so that it
slots into the decoration of
the complete wall.

Here the window has
been virtually boxed in on all
sides by shelves as well as a
narrow table (which opens
out into a dining table). The
stripes of the roller blind
echo the room's colour
scheme and upholstery
fabric, and co-ordinate with
the objects displayed on the
shelves.

◁ **Filtered light**
Floor-to-ceiling pinoleum
blinds filter light attractively,
creating a rich glow in this
living room.

Traditionally made from
fine strips of wood woven
together with cotton,
pinoleum blinds are now also
made from plastic in a range
of colours. Such blinds do
have one disadvantage –
they can be seen through at
night.

A SIMPLE APPROACH

If you don't want the windows to dominate your room, there are two approaches you can adopt.

First, use a plain treatment. Make simple curtains from a self-patterned weave, perhaps, in a neutral shade or one which blends with the room's colour scheme, to produce curtains which are elegant but not dominant. Similarly, roller or roman blinds can merge into the background.

An alternative approach is to dress the windows so that they become an integral part of the overall scheme. This sometimes means choosing a bright colour or strong pattern which is used in relatively large quantities near the windows. If, for example, the curtain fabric matches the wallpaper, even floor-length curtains will not stand out from the walls which flank them.

Dressing down your windows need not mean boring windows – merely a carefully-chosen approach that blends with the overall decor.

△ *All white*
Deceptively simple curtains merge with the white walls, carpet and furniture around them. The plain fabric and straightforward treatment combine to produce curtains which add a note of serene elegance to this calm and restful decorating scheme.

The curtains are gathered several inches from the top, and hang from a wooden pole on extra-large rings.

In such a pale colour scheme which is not relieved by patterned fabrics or extra colours, the wooden curtain poles and furniture play a vital role in preventing the atmosphere from becoming monotonous. The curtain poles also define the top of the windows in relation to the sloping and irregular ceiling.

BRIGHT IDEA

Alternatives to net Roller or roman blinds made from a sheer fabric provide up-to-date alternatives to traditional net curtains. Such blinds provide shade and privacy, hide an ugly view and still allow light to penetrate. The material which is used can be plain or patterned.

▷ *Extravaganza in red*
The rich glowing austrian blinds covering these picture windows create a blaze of fiery colour. The frills and deep flounces provide a dramatic contrast to the relatively severe, Japanese-style furniture. Such blinds would be equally at home in a more traditional environment – so long as competing colour and pattern is kept to a minimum.

▽ *Dressing a bay window*
The frilled edges of the full curtains which cover this bay turn the window into an impressive feature.

To accentuate the shape of the window recess, the curtains are segmented into four, each of which is gathered by a tieback. A translucent roller blind can be pulled down over each window by means of a heavy tassel.

STYLES OF WINDOW DRESSING

There are so many different ways to dress a window that you could find yourself spoilt for choice.

The way you dress your windows, with curtains, blinds, shutters or a combination of these, is a matter of personal taste. Traditional Georgian windows can look unexpectedly stylish with stark, modern venetian blinds, or modern windows in a brand new home can be given the Victorian treatment with heavy drapes, frilled valances, and lace curtains or roller blinds.

It is normally the overall furnishing style of the room which dictates your final choice; a room furnished in an English country house style would look odd if the windows were clothed with nothing but roller blinds.

However, there may be certain difficulties which prevent you from choosing a particular style: it can be difficult to fit a traditional wooden pole round a bay or bow window, for example; and if you have a deeply recessed cottage window, you want to make sure you get all the light you can, so a droopy, austrian blind is probably an inappropriate choice.

Since there are absolutely no hard and fast rules for designing window dressings, you can mix and match all sorts of different ideas, combining them as you want or replacing them with shutters or blinds to create just the right atmosphere for the room which you are decorating.

Whichever style you choose in the end, don't forget the basic rules for hanging curtains:
● decide on a style and fit the track or pole before measuring up
● don't hang curtains so that they cover radiators under windows at night
● try to avoid cutting out light, particularly when hanging curtains at small windows.

CURTAIN STYLES

 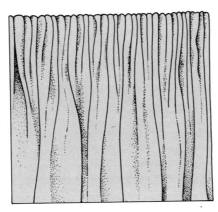 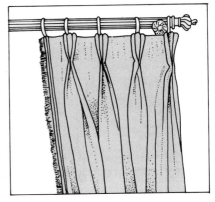

STRAIGHT CURTAINS
Style The simplest approach to dressing your window is to hang straight curtains. These can either be bought ready-made, or can be made to measure for your window using either heading tapes or hand-made headings.

The most common finishes which are used with exposed headings include pencil pleats (above centre), triple pinch pleats (above right) or cartridge pleats. You can choose virtually any fabric for your curtains – from fine sheer voiles to heavy velvets.

In use Curtains may be hung so the track is either exposed or covered, but this will depend on the position of the hooks in the heading tape. When you are combining pinch pleats with either wooden or brass rings, you should always position the hooks at the centre of each pleat.

Don't let the size of your windows restrict your selection when you are deciding on a suitable curtain style for your window – you can create illusions by making curtains larger than the windows: a wide, shallow window looks more imposing with a ceiling-to-floor treatment; a narrow window can be made to look much wider by extending the track on either side of the window.

Watchpoint If you have a window sill which protrudes, hang the curtains from a track or pole which is fixed on brackets so that the curtain falls away from the sill. Alternatively hang the curtains so that they only reach the level of the sill.

CASED HEADINGS
Style Cased headings can be an economical way to hang curtains and valances as you don't need gliders, hooks and heading tape. A casing is stitched at the top and just slots on to a rod, pole, or expanding curtain wire (reverse side shown, near right).

This type of heading may be used on elaborate, lined curtains, or just as successfully on simple unlined or sheer curtains. A cased heading on a chunky pole looks good at the top of an austrian blind, and holds the blind firmly in place when in use. When using this style for small, unlined curtains, a frilled edge to the casing adds a soft detail.

Some manufacturers produce quite wide valance tracks and these can be used to make a substantial cased heading. Fitted on to swivel rods, this style can be used successfully for dormer windows as well.

In use Curtains which have cased headings are really meant to be left closed at the top. In daylight or when necessary, they can be held back with tiebacks.

Watchpoint If curtains with cased headings are fixed to glazed doors or pivot window frames, then it is a good idea to fit expanded curtain wire or fine rods to the top and bottom so that the curtains do not catch when they are opened.

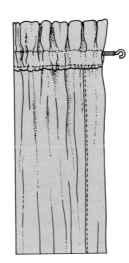 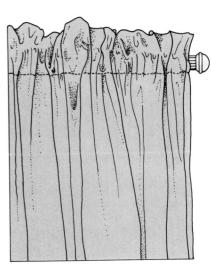

TIEBACKS

Style Tiebacks are a practical and decorative addition to curtains and enable you to let more light into your room during the day whilst still creating an elaborate draped effect.

There are many different types of tiebacks: simple tasselled cords can be bought ready-made, and some ready-made curtains are available with matching frilled tiebacks.

However, if you make your own tiebacks or have them made-to-measure, you will find that the range of styles is much more extensive – straight, shaped, bound edged, frilled, ruched, or plaited styles can all be made. The fabric that you use can match or contrast with the curtain fabric.

In use Tiebacks can be positioned either low down or high up the curtain to create the look you want. To give your windows an American look, put the tiebacks high up the window, so that the curtains are held well apart. For a heavily-draped effect, with curtains which tumble down to the floor, make long tiebacks and position them low down the window. When this elaborate, draped effect has been created, tiebacks are usually left permanently in position and the curtains are not closed at night.

Watchpoint Avoid using tiebacks with velvet curtains as they crush the pile and spoil the look of the curtains.

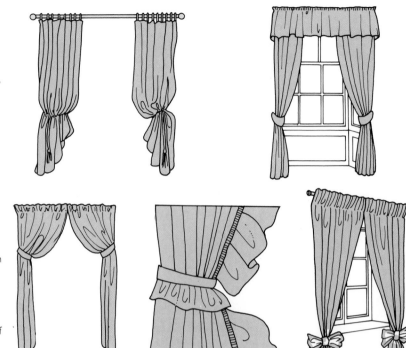

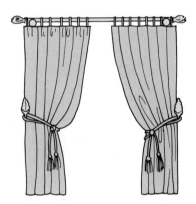

HOLDBACKS

Style Simple or decorative knobs and brackets which are used to hold curtains away from the window. If preferred, you can also use them instead of discreet hooks to hold your tiebacks in position (left). They can be used to create unusual draped effects with your curtains too.

In use Unless holdbacks are used with tiebacks they are not really suitable for bulky curtains as they won't hold them in place properly.

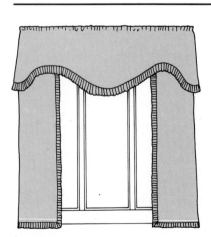

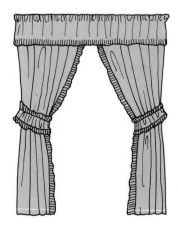

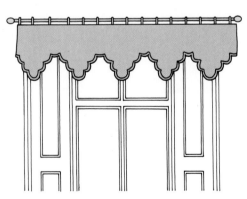

VALANCES

Style Elaborate, soft fabric panels which are placed at the top of windows. Valances can have bound edges and be shaped and/or frilled. They look particularly effective in glazed cottons and chintzes above full, straight or gathered curtains in the English country house style.

In use Traditionally, valances are combined with curtains, and are hung from a valance track or a pelmet shelf. Some styles simply slot on to a narrow or wide valance track.

Valances can, of course, be hung on their own, without accompanying curtains, from a curtain pole for a fresh effect in a kitchen or bathroom.

Alternatively, they can be combined with either shutters, café curtains or blinds.

Watchpoint If you do not have large windows, hang the valance so that its lower edge is only slightly below the top of the window if possible. This will prevent the valance from cutting out any light.

PELMETS

Style These are like valances but are wooden or stiff card panels covered in fabric which are positioned over the curtain heading. The fabric may be extravagantly shaped, and can be trimmed with braid and fringing. You can also improvise with carved panels, or embroidered braids which you can buy from oriental markets.

In use As well as being decorative, a pelmet helps to keep tops of curtains clean, as well as bridging the unsightly gap between the ceiling and the top of the window.

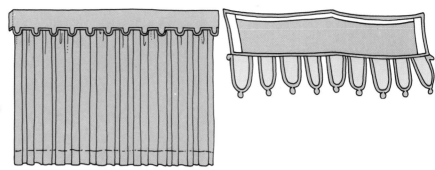

SWAGS AND TAILS

Swags and tails are the most elaborate way of adding extra elegance to windows and covering curtain headings. But they are expensive to buy ready-made and difficult to sew by yourself. Formal swags sweep across the top of the window, with tails hanging in pleats down the sides. Contrast linings and/or binding, braids and fringes can all be used to add ornate touches to your window dressing.

In use Fit swags and tails to a pelmet shelf, combined with straight or tied-back curtains, or use them with lace curtains and/or blinds for privacy at night.

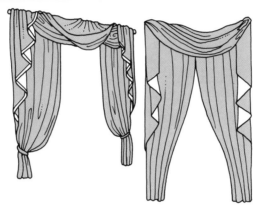

DRAPED STYLES

Style Swags of fabric which are draped over poles or brackets above the window to create an informal up-to-the-minute look. This style of window dressing can imitate full curtains, or replace swags and tails. For economy, keep these styles simple and use budget fabrics such as coloured lining, calico or mattress ticking. Create a fantasy effect with muslin or Terylene sheers, or add a lavish touch by letting fabric tumble to the floor.

In use Swagged drapes cannot be closed at night so hang plain curtains from a separate track, fitted closer to the window than the drapes, or add a fairly plain roman or roller blind.

Watchpoint Use Velcro tabs to anchor the drapes in place.

ASYMMETRIC STYLES

Style Popular in the 18th century, these styles are now enjoying a revival. They are simply a matter of letting your imagination run riot, and experimenting with lengths of fabric until you achieve the right effect. Curtains and swags and tails can be draped across the window and held in place with tiebacks. Asymmetric styles are particularly useful if a window is awkwardly positioned in a corner; they also look good on pairs of windows, either next to each other or opposite, so that the arrangement is mirrored. Asymmetric styles can also create simple, rustic effects (with panels of voile or lace draped over poles) or stylishly modern looks.

In use Usually made up as dress curtains, with blinds beneath. You may need to fit special brackets which hold several tracks to create a layered effect.

Watchpoint Extravagant effects usually demand rich, expensive fabrics.

CAFÉ CURTAINS AND COMBINATIONS

Style Café curtains are hung to screen the lower part of the window, and are usually left permanently closed.

They can be made up with a gathered heading tape, a cased heading, or a scalloped heading, and hung from rods or poles, with or without rings. The rods or poles are usually fixed mid-way up the window but this can vary to suit your personal taste and needs. If there are glazing bars on the window, try to install the fixing level with one of them.

In use Cafés may look a bit skimpy on their own: if so, make up a combination by adding a valance, curtain, or blind.

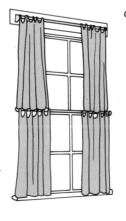

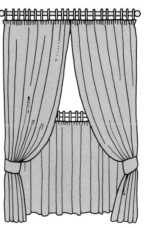

CLEVER DETAILS

Style Panels of fabric may be hung from a pole using clip-on curtain rings (far right). Attach the rings so that the top edge of the panel falls forwards, adding extra interest.

For an alternative look, combine American style holdbacks with a more modern touch such as a brightly coloured venetian blind (right).

For a cheap but opulent effect, cover the wall containing the window with fabric and use a holdback to allow light to enter (centre right).

BAY AND BOW WINDOWS

Styles Your choice of window dressing may be limited if you have bay or bow windows, since some types of track or pole will not go round the corners.

You can emphasize architectural style with roman or roller blinds, or fit tracks which will curve right around the bay. On larger bays, you can stack the curtains at the angles, leaving them to hang straight or holding them clear of the windows with tiebacks, but on smaller bays it is better to draw the curtains clear of the window and round into the room if possible.

In use A simple solution is to fit a pole or track across the bay window to create a recess. Some bay and bow windows look especially good with a wooden or brass pole and a simple curtain hung across the opening, with sheer blinds at the windows.

Often, though, dress curtains are the best solution in a bay, particularly if there are radiators under the window.

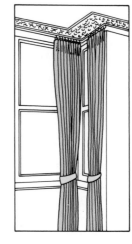

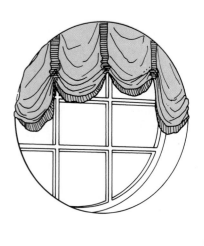

UNUSUALLY-SHAPED WINDOWS

Style Round windows (above, far right) and those with arched or pointed tops need special consideration to avoid detracting from their shape. An attractive solution is to fit curtains or blinds inside the recess (with Velcro, or by hanging them from screw eyes) or arrange them so that they hang well clear of the window.

In use Fitting curtains inside the recess may mean that you lose a lot of light during the day. High tiebacks will help to keep the curtains clear of the window.

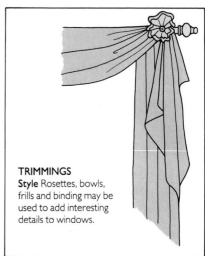

TRIMMINGS

Style Rosettes, bowls, frills and binding may be used to add interesting details to windows.

CURTAIN HEADINGS

The headings you choose for your curtains add the finishing touch to your window dressing.

Curtain headings, as distinct from pelmets and valances, come in many different styles, from the formal and imposing to the casual and informal. The simplest style is a gathered heading made with commercial tape. At the other end of the scale, cartridge or goblet headings must be hand sewn as there is no commercial tape that does the job.

Pencil-pleated curtains are very popular, along with their more sophisticated relation, the pinch-pleated curtain, which is making something of a comeback. Although commercial heading tapes are available for both styles, purists assert that hand-finished pinch-pleated curtains are infinitely superior to their ready-made counterparts.

Bearing in mind that the large amount of fabric required entails not inconsiderable expense, it is worthwhile taking a little more time and trouble to do the work by hand and attain a perfect end result. This is especially true where you are using heavy fabric, lining and interlining, because a hand-sewn heading can be made sufficiently stiff to support the weight and bulk of the curtains and avoid unsightly sagging.

There are three standard fittings for hanging curtains: an exposed pole, with rings (usually finished in brass, or natural or painted wood), curtain tracks and rails (either plastic or metal), and poles (or rods) inserted through a channel at the top of the curtain (used for cased headings and café curtains).

BRIGHT IDEA

All tied up If you've a window that's overlooked, why not try something more interesting than an ordinary net curtain? This sheer fabric with a spotted design has a simple gathered heading attached to the curtain pole by lengths of ribbon. These can be easily stitched on to the reverse of the heading tape. Here, the ribbons have been carefully chosen to match the spots in the wallpaper.

◁ *A perfect pair*
A pair of pencil-pleated curtains has a gathered frill on their leading edge. Made from a bright and cheerful cotton fabric, they hang from a simple white curtain pole and rings that echo both the paintwork and the stripe in the wallpaper. The more gently gathered austrian blind is made of a striped, co-ordinating fabric, and hangs from a standard track. Notice how the headings of the curtains and blind are at exactly the same height, despite the different fixings.
The gathered frill at the lower edge of the blind is piped in a matching plain blue fabric. The curtain tiebacks; made in the same fabric as the blind, are bound and tied with the same plain fabric.

▷ Dressed for effect

This lavishly curtained bay window makes an elegant setting for a small dining table. Rich, pinch-pleated dress curtains are made of a pale golden fabric, which is also used on the leading edge of the under-curtain and for the tailored tablecloth. Pinch-pleated (or French-pleated) curtains need fabric two and a half times the length of the track in order to hang really well. This pair looks especially luxurious because the curtains have been interlined as well as lined.

In the interests of economy, the pinch-pleated under-curtains are made out of good quality lining fabric. This is now available in a wide range of colours, making it a useful material where the required effect calls for plenty of fabric. The alternative is to skimp on the quantity of fabric needed (which can look terrible), but here nothing detracts from the sense of grandeur: a feeling reinforced by hanging the curtain from the very top of the wall, not simply from the top of the window.

Two curtain tracks were fitted, the top one for the dress curtains, and the second one for the under-curtains, which can be pulled back during the day.

◁ Buttoned up

Simple and stylish, these off-white curtains promote a feeling of cool elegance. The heading is finished with buttons – in other words, pinch-pleated curtains have had buttons sewn on to the pleats, thus they have a 'buttoned heading'. In this case, the buttons are covered in the patterned edging fabric and so draw attention to the neat pinch pleats. At the same time, by drawing the eye upwards, the heading emphasizes the height of the room. The border, which runs along the bottom of the curtains and up both sides, is co-ordinated with the sofa upholstery fabric, injecting colour and defining the edges of the curtain against the off-white wall. Dark wood rings and a curtain rail, fixed on a bracket so as to project beyond the edge of the window frame, are a simple yet sophisticated device for hanging pinch-pleated curtains.

▷ **Squared up**
A straight looped heading gives a castellated effect to this contrast-lined curtain. As with café curtains, the loops are an extension of the curtain, formed at the cutting out stage, and not just attached later. The allowance for the loops is twice the distance between the curtain heading and the pole, plus enough to go round the pole, and 2½cm to fold under and sew on to the back of the curtain. To calculate the amount of fabric, allow roughly 1½ times the width by the drop plus the hem and length of loops. With fine attention to detail, the castellations make a feature of the pattern on the loops.

▽ **Over the top**
These curtains are stiffened at the top with a dress stiffener, while an extra-deep turning makes an eye-catching heading. Hooks for the curtain rings are sewn on by hand, some way down the curtain (in this case about 10cm below the top edge). The use of a pole and curtain rings complements the simplicity and informality of this style of curtain heading.

△ **Sheer delight**
Sheer fabrics, being less expensive, are ideal for generous window dressings. This treatment calls for 2½ times the window width in both fabrics. The top fabric is split in two vertically and hemmed along the leading edges. The two fabrics are then tacked together at the top and turned over to form an 18cm hem. Pencil pleat heading tape is attached 5cm below the top edge. When gathered up the top 5cm forms a frill. Plaited tiebacks and trim complete the picture.

△ Corner slot

Cased headings are ideal for light curtains that aren't drawn to and fro, but still need a generous quantity of fabric. For the heading, turn over 2.5cm and a further 7.5cm. To form the casing, make two lines of stitching sufficiently far apart to accept the diameter of your pole. As you slip the casing on to the pole, distribute the fullness evenly.

▷ Goblet pleats

Formal and smart, these are a variation of pinch pleats. On these imposing curtains, matching rope has been knotted to coincide with the base of each pleat.

◁ Simple elegance

If you prefer to use a standard ready-made curtain heading, you can still achieve an elegant and stylish effect. Here, an ordinary pair of curtains have been transformed by the addition of extravagant, softly draped swags framing the top of the window. A matching tablecloth and braided tiebacks complete the picture.

UNUSUAL CURTAIN TIEBACKS

Finish off a classic English look
with an unusual tieback, or adapt
our designs to create your own.

Interior designers who favour the English country style are developing more and more extravagant looks for windows: over-sized, padded curtains, frilled and flounced valances and softly-tied or puffy tiebacks that add a casual, yet planned and co-ordinated touch to a formal look.

Tiebacks take little fabric, so you can afford to experiment with some of the new styles. They are rather more elaborate than most tailored tiebacks, so if you're apprehensive about the final effect, follow the detailed instructions for one of the three styles shown here – a softer tie, a plait or a puffy bow. For the traditional English look, choose chintz.

CHOOSE YOUR FABRICS

Mix and match plain and patterned chintzes in the same weight for extra interest. Moiré silks are suitable for more formal settings, but do choose fabrics that tie in with others in the room: if, for example, you already have a set of curtains, and can't match the fabric exactly, buy a selection of plain, toning fabrics, and use them to make up tiebacks and a valance for the curtains. Then use additional lengths of the fabric for cushions or over-cloths for circular tables elsewhere in the room to balance the dressy windows.

MEASURING UP

If you can afford to lose some light at your window, long tiebacks and heavily-gathered curtains will ensure an elegant effect. Shorter tiebacks are better for small windows, giving a more cottagey look. Use a tape measure to judge the finished length of the tiebacks, holding it in place to loop the curtains to the sides of the window.

It is important to look at the length of the curtains at the same time: sometimes, the addition of tiebacks to drape the curtain fabric will lift the hem of the curtain so far off the floor that instead of producing a luxurious effect the overall look is skimped. Interior designers tend to use these more decorative tiebacks with curtains which tumble on to the floor so that even when tied back the curtains look luxurious. In some cases you may find it more practical to use tiebacks with curtains that are shaped at the hems, so that when tied back the hem is just a centimetre or so above floor level. In this case, you will have to regard the curtains as dress curtains, permanently tied back, since the shaped hems will trail unevenly on the ground when the curtains are closed and the neat effect given when the curtains are tied back is completely lost.

Once you have measured up, calculate the amount of fabric you need, following the instructions for each style of tieback.

Plait it rich
The length of the tieback, the thickness of the plait and the elegance of the striped curtain fabric add up to a look that is both formal and luxurious in this living room.

A SOFTLY TIED, PIPED TIEBACK

This style of tieback, made from a simple length of fabric and piped at the edges, adds an informal touch to your windows.

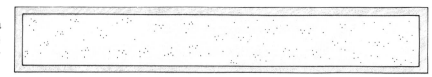

1 Calculate the amount of fabric

These tiebacks are cut from strips of fabric 15cm deep, plus 3cm·for seam allowances. The length is the measured length of the finished tieback, plus about 45cm for making the tie. Add 3cm seam allowance for a piped finish. You will need the same amount of fabric to line the tieback, in matching or contrasting fabric.

Calculate the amount of piping (twice the length plus twice the depth of the tieback), adding 1.5cm seam allowance for joining the ends. Use ready-made bias binding, or cut your own, 3.5cm wide, cut on the cross. You need the same amount of fine piping cord.

2 Cut out the fabric

For each tieback cut a strip of fabric, adding 1.5cm allowances for a piped finish. A good finished length is 1.20m, so the tiebacks can be cut across the width of most furnishing fabrics. Cut same-sized strips to line the tiebacks. If you are not using a crisp fabric, cut strips of lightweight iron-on interfacing the exact size of the finished tieback. Cut bias strips for piping if necessary.

3 Interface the tiebacks △

To give the tiebacks extra body, you can interface them with a lightweight iron-on interfacing. Lay out the main piece of fabric wrong side up and position iron-on interfacing on it: leave a 1.5cm border all round the interfacing for a piped finish. Iron on the interfacing according to the manufacturer's instructions to bond it to the fabric.

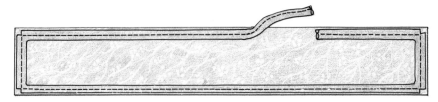

CHECK YOUR NEEDS
- ☐ Suitable fabrics (chintzes, moiré)
- ☐ Tape measure
- ☐ Sewing thread
- ☐ Scissors
- ☐ Pins and needles
- ☐ Piping and binding (optional)
- ☐ Lightweight iron-on interfacing (optional)
- ☐ Wadding (optional)
- ☐ Paper for pattern (optional)
- ☐ Rings and hooks to hold tiebacks

4 Prepare the piping △

Make up the piping to fit round the tieback, allowing extra for joining. Position the piping ensuring that the seamline of the piping matches the seamline of the fabric. Pin and tack in place. Join ends of piping by unwinding the strands at each end and trimming each strand to a slightly different length and entwine. At the corners, notch the seam allowance of the binding so that it lies flat. Machine stitch in place.

5 Add the lining

Position the lining over the fabric and the piping, right sides facing, so that the raw edges match. Pin and tack in place, then stitch close to the stitching line on piping, leaving a 10cm opening halfway down one long side of the tieback. Press stitching, clip seam allowance at corners and turn right side out. Press again, then slipstitch the lining to the seam allowance of the piping along opening to close up and make a neat finish.

6 Attach the rings

Tie the tiebacks round the curtains and hold the tieback against the window frame so you can judge where the hook to hold the tieback should be fixed, and where the ring should be attached to the tieback. (If you attach the ring to the exact centre of one long edge of the tieback, you may find that one end hangs down further than the other when you make the soft knot.)

If the window surround is wood, use a cuphook, making a small hole with a bradawl first. You will have to drill and fit a wall plug if there is a plaster finish where the tieback is to be fixed.

Sew a curtain ring to the middle of each short edge. Working on the wrong side of the fabric, slightly overcast the ring inside the edge so that it fits over the hook.

◁ Soft and simple
This pair of tiebacks really do 'tie' the curtain in place. Here, straight pieces of fabric are cut out, lined and piped in a contrast colour.

PLAITED TIEBACKS

Squashy plaited tiebacks in a mixture of fabrics add a distinctive touch and underline the colours you want to emphasize in a room. The strands are padded with heavyweight polyester wadding to give an extravagant-looking finish.

Decide on the finished length of the tieback, then decide how many strands you want to make up the plait. Three is the usual number for plaits, but in this case we have used five strands. You could also use four or six strands – experiment with remnants of fabric to test the effect.

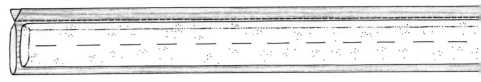

1 Calculate and cut out fabric
Each strand is made from a 10cm wide strip of fabric, padded with a 3cm wide strip of wadding. Make each strip twice the finished length of the tieback (i.e. for a 60cm tieback, cut strips 120cm long). Cut five strips of fabric, the appropriate length and 10cm wide. Cut five strips of wadding, 3cm wide. Save remnants for binding the ends.

2 Make up the strands △
For each strand, position the wadding on the wrong side of the fabric, 1.75cm from one raw edge of the fabric. Tack in place. Fold the fabric in half lengthwise, right sides together so raw edges match. Pin, tack and stitch 1.5cm from raw edge. Turn tube the right side out. Remove tacking. Press lightly, without crushing wadding.

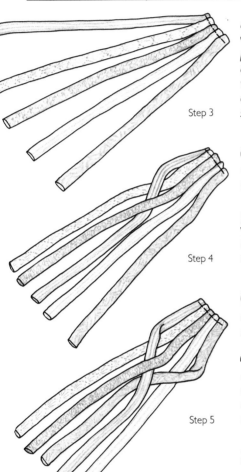

Step 3

Step 4

Step 5

3 Arrange the strands ◁
Lay the five strands out on a table, positioning them so that each strand overlaps the next by about half its width. Pin and tack together across one end. The plaiting is easier if you can ask someone to hold the end.

4 Start to plait from left ◁
Take the left-hand strand and weave it over the strand next to it, then under the centre strand.

5 Plait from right ◁
Next take the strand on the right and weave it over the strand next to it and under the strand now in the centre.

6 Fold over right-hand strand ▷
Now take the right-hand strand and fold it over to make a neat edge, laying over the strand next to it.

7 Make the plait ▷
Continue by taking the left-hand strand, turning it over at right angles to make a neat edge, then weaving over, under and over the next three strands.

8 Repeat the step
Repeat the last two steps until you have made a plait slightly longer than the finished tie-back.

Step 6

Step 7

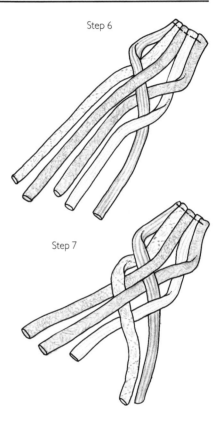

9 Adjust the strands
When you have made the plait, check the effect: the plait should be even and firm – undo it and start again if you are not happy with the look.

10 Neaten the ends ▽
When you are happy with the effect, tack firmly across each end of the plait, 1.5cm from where you want to make the end of the tieback. Trim the fabric 1.5cm from the line of tacking.

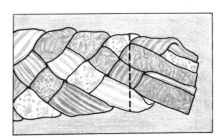

11 Bind the ends ▷
For each end, cut a piece of fabric the width of the tieback plus 3cm seam allowance, and 6cm long. Position it on the tieback, right sides facing and raw edges matching. Stitch in place across tieback, 1.5cm from end. Press binding strip towards end of tieback and fold under 1.5cm across end. Then fold under 1.5cm down each side.

12 Slipstitch binding
Fold binding over end of tieback, and pin tack and slipstitch across back and down sides. Attach rings to end.

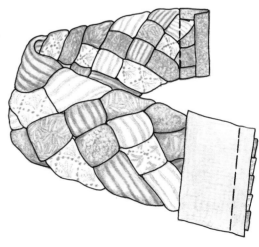

ADDING A BOW

A puffy bow adds a fashionable, femi-nine touch to a straight tieback.

1 **Calculate the amount of fabric**
For each bow, you will need a strip of fabric 60cm long by 30cm wide, plus a strip 10cm long by 16cm wide. Cut a piece of interfacing 12cm wide by 54cm long.

2 **Cut out and interface bow** △
Cut out the fabric. If it is not a crisp fabric, add interfacing. Position interfacing on wrong side of fabric

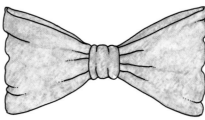

down the centre of the strip. Press in place, following manufacturer's instructions. Make a 1cm double hem all round each section.

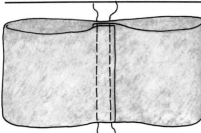

3 **Make the loops** △
With wrong sides of fabric facing, fold the larger strip softly down each side so that the edges meet down the centre. Fold the ends of the strip to the centre, so they overlap by 2cm. Do not press, as the aim is to achieve a soft, puffy effect. Make two lines of gathering stitches, between the two ends, through all layers of fabric.

4 **Make the knot** △
Draw up the gathers so that the loops of the bow puff out. Fold the fabric for the knot so that the sides meet down the centre, to make a piece 6cm square. Wrap it round the centre of the bow, bunching it to create a knot. Pin and tack the ends together at the back. Stitch by hand, taking care not to stitch through the front of the knot.

5 **Attach to the tieback**
Make up the tieback and fix it in place. Pin the bow to the tieback before stitching by hand.

BRIGHT IDEA

TAKE A BOW

Co-ordinate your tiebacks and valance by adding matching bows along the top of the valance. Make up the bows exactly as described for the tiebacks, and make up a valance with a gathered heading. Stitch bows to the valance every 40-50cm across the width of the window.

◁ **Puff-ball bows**
The final, feminine touch in this bedroom is the addition of a bow to ordinary straight tiebacks. With a crisp, glazed cotton it is not necessary to interline the fabric.

CURTAIN PELMETS AND VALANCES

Whether you opt for formal and imposing pelmets, or informal and soft valances, they will add a stylish finishing touch.

The difference between a pelmet and a valance is not only the grandeur of the end result but also the construction, the way the fabric is used and the fixing. Pelmets are generally rigid, stiff and firmly attached to a projecting fixing board. Valances are usually gently draped, less structured and softer in appearance.

Pelmets and valances are usually combined with curtains, but this is a modern assumption: historically, they were often combined with blinds. By the 17th century there were two types of blinds: one was a piece of fabric, mounted on wooden battens and fixed into the window recess, the other was an early version of the festoon blind.

Single curtains date back to the 17th century, but divided curtains were rarely used until the end of the century.

'Capping' first appeared in the late 17th century. A shaped or scalloped pelmet, it ran over the top of the windows and around the room, neatening or even eliminating the join between the wall or window and the ceiling. The French or Empire style of lavishly draped pelmets and valances originated in the late 18th century, and drapery remained popular until well into the 19th century and the start of the Arts and Crafts movement. Roller blinds made their first appearance around 1830, shortly after internally-sprung upholstery was developed.

Although pelmets are normally covered with fabric, this need not always be the case. Curtains can be hung behind a cornice or the architrave of the window itself, in which case the pelmet is in fact made of plaster in the first instance and wood in the second. Cornice pelmets are a refined, architecturally pleasing detail.

Grand gestures

A large bay window has been dressed to maximum effect, with under-curtains, dress curtains, tails and a pleated pelmet in front of the under-curtains to match the knife-edge pleats at the heading of the dress curtains.

Three co-ordinating fabrics have been used: the first in the dress curtains, the second in the under-curtains and the lining of the tails, and the third in the tails, the window seat cushions and the pleated infills below.

The grandeur of this window is largely due to the generous quantities of fabric, from the dress curtains which flow on to the floor, to the pinch-pleated under-curtains which have, more unusually, been left long to fall on to the window seat. The wooden pelmet has been painted white to match the cornice and the window frame.

△ A simple swag

The floor, french windows and curtain pole have been lightly stained and varnished, creating a perfect setting for this deceptively simple window dressing. It is made in two stages. First a length of fabric is draped along the curtain pole, arranged to form a swag and fixed with Velcro. The dress curtains are attached separately, and are puffed out on the floor, away from the doors. Where the swag meets the dress curtains, a puff-ball (made by gathering up and lightly stuffing a circular piece of fabric) has been attached. Matching roller blinds have been fixed to each of the doors.

△ Scalloped valances

The valances for the bed and the window have been made to match. By fixing the window dressing to a curved pelmet shelf, it echoes the semi-circular half-tester. The valance is cut out in generous scallop shapes, lined with a co-ordinating fabric, and tightly gathered on to pencil-pleated heading tape. Contrast binding has been applied to neatly finish the top and bottom of the heading and add definition to the contours of the scallops.

The bed curtains have been lined with a co-ordinating fabric, while the main fabric has been diamond-quilted and made into a bedspread to complete the scheme.

◁ A fishy fantasy

Printed fabric with an ikat design has been used for the curtains and pelmet in this elaborate window treatment. Each 'fish scale' has been made by covering a stiffened template with a piece of fabric, carefully planned and cut to show the same section of pattern on every piece. The pelmet has been meticulously assembled to fit exactly, resulting in a spectacular and original, if time-consuming, window dressing.

▷ Simple stripes

A straight pelmet and a pair of curtains with rope tiebacks might sound traditional – even a little old-fashioned. But in this case, nothing could be farther from the truth. Charcoal and white striped fabric, plain white fabric and two lengths of simple, silver grey rope have been combined to create the antithesis of an over-ornate and heavy window dressing.

The use of different fabrics for the two curtains gives the window a stylish asymmetrical appearance. Using the stripes horizontally rather than vertically on the pelmet creates a highly effective and slightly surprising result, one which is totally in keeping with a stark and modern scheme.

▽ Swagged box pleats

This elaborate valance is not for the novice curtain-maker! Two fabrics are combined to make a box-pleated valance, which is then partly gathered up between the pleats in the manner of an austrian blind. Notice the attention to details such as the half swags on the returns of the valance and the variations in the length of the swags, which are carefully balanced from the centre towards the sides.

△ A scenic bay

A large, rectangular bay window has been dressed with floor-length curtains, unobtrusively tied to obstruct as little light as possible. The pelmet has been cut out with a layer of buckram to stiffen it, and trimmed with braid. It runs round the three sides of the bay and has scallops of alternating width and depth to add interest to what could become a monotonous rhythm.

▷ Frills and flounces

Two gentle arcs along the lower edge mean this symmetrical valance is slightly longer in the middle, where it forms a cornet. At the sides the fabric has been left twice as long, and encouraged to fall into tails. The frill which runs along the bottom of the valance gives added weight and emphasizes the shape and sumptuous atmosphere.

Positioning the gathering slightly below the top edge of the valance gives a frilled effect. The orange fabric used for the austrian blind has been cut on the bias to bind the top edge of the valance, the piping along the top of the frill, and the binding of the lower edge of the frill. It has also been used to line the valance, as it is visible on the central cornet and the side tails. Three bows decorate the middle and sides of the valance.

The full length dress curtains have a bound leading edge, and matching orange fabric has been used to cover the walls and the scatter cushions, all of which combine to create a sumptuous and opulent living room.

◁ Fringe benefits

A range of wallpapers, borders and fabrics have been used sympathetically in this room. Co-ordinating collections are ideal for this type of elaborate treatment as they remain gentle on the eye. Here, the same pattern has been used for the swags, tails and tiebacks. Another pattern has been used for the curtains, but this does not make the window treatment feel fussy as both patterns contain the same colours. Instead of using a contrasting fabric to line the tails, restraint has been exercised, and they are self-lined. A grey fringe is the only extravagance.

CURTAINS FOR CURVED WINDOWS

Unusual and interesting windows have their disadvantages, but offer the adventurous a wealth of opportunities.

Arched, curved or round windows are splendid architectural details and, as such, should be treated with respect. They will certainly stretch your sewing skills when it comes to making curtains but should also fire your imagination. A porthole window, for instance, is reminiscent of many things, most of which have little to do with a view over the back garden. This, in part, is the magic of unusually shaped windows, and is why they deserve to be dressed with extra care and attention to detail.

There are two distinctly different approaches to curved, arched or round windows. The first of these two methods disregards the shape of the window, and involves fixing a simple pole or track straight across the top. When drawn back, the curtains hang well clear, and don't obstruct the light.

The second approach takes into account the shape of the window, so that the blind, curtain and/or pelmet treatment both reflects and complements the shape.

There are two ways of fixing curtains so that they follow the curve of an arched window. A flexible aluminium curtain track can be bent by the manufacturer or supplier to a template of the arch. Then, instead of using gliders, endstops are positioned at strategic intervals, and the curtains are hung from these. This track has to be fixed inside the reveal of the arch.

The alternative is to fix a wooden batten outside the arch, and use screweyes. Whichever method you opt for, the curtains will not draw, and must be hooked or tied back when not in use.

Net effects
Above the french doors, a rectangular piece of net, up to twice the length of the arc, had narrow heading tape fixed to the two long edges. It was then gathered to fit the arch and stapled into position. The lower curtains were pleated and attached to a light track.

△ **Underneath the arches**
Plywood, cut to the same profile as the windows, has been fixed above the arches. Screw-eyes hold the pencil-pleated silk curtains in place. Contrasting fabric, draped to form swags, is bunched up at picture rail height and falls into tails. The asymmetrical treatment of the two outer windows results in a pleasing balance over the wall as a whole.

▽ **Undisturbed view**
This living room needs neither curtains nor nets as it cannot be overlooked. To soften the dramatic windows, curtain poles have been draped with fabric. Used in sufficient quantity, the fabric falls down to the raised area, forming graceful dress curtains. The neutral colours in the fabric help to pull the whole scheme together.

△ Defying gravity

The treatment of this unusual bay window arrangement neatly overcomes the problem of being overlooked by other houses. Roller blinds are used at night for privacy, but during the day they are hidden from sight. Fixed along the back of the window seat, behind the cushions, the blinds are pulled up at dusk and hooked on to the glazing bars just below the top of the arched windows. By using a stiffener, it would be possible to match the blinds to the fabric that lines the bay window.

▽ On the right track

The diagram shows a flexible aluminium track bent to the arc of the window. By taking a template of your arched window, manufacturers or suppliers can bend the track to order, so that it fits the curve perfectly. Gliders or runners would not work in this situation, so endstops are used along the length of the track instead, as they won't slip down to the lowest point. Curtains are hooked on to these in the usual way. As they then can't be drawn back, they must be hooked or tied back.

Disguising an ugly view does not necessitate obscuring a pretty window. Curtains and blinds get dirty in a kitchen, so plants, positioned on fitted glass shelves, will hide the outlook.

◁ *A pretty porthole*
A french or pinch-pleated valance has been painstakingly constructed to echo the contours of this round window. This idea could be copied with a plain pelmet or another style of valance. Here, the piped and frilled lower edge enhances the shapely curve of the window and matches the tiebacks.

▽ *More ways with arched windows*
The staggered austrian blind on the left pulls up to emphasize the arched window. The curtains at the french windows (centre) are held back at the bottom of the arch, again emphasizing its shape. The approach shown on the right is modern, with fine venetian blinds that are barely noticeable when open.

BLINDS FOR ATMOSPHERE

Whether sleek and tailored or frilled and flounced, blinds are the fashionable treatment for a well-dressed window.

Roller blinds date back to Victorian times, venetian blinds became fashionable in the 1950s, but festoon and austrian blinds were rarely seen more than 15 years ago. Nowadays, improved central heating and double glazing have eliminated the necessity for heavy curtains, traditionally both lined and interlined, which minimized those uncomfortable draughts associated with ill-fitting windows.

As blinds became increasingly popular, manufacturers responded to the demand and swiftly produced a wide range of DIY kits for roller, roman,

austrian and festoon blinds. Horizontal and vertical louvres must be ordered to the dimensions of your windows, and are supplied ready to fix.

The atmosphere you want to create obviously influences your decision, but with very expensive fabrics, consider dressing the window with blinds instead of curtains. As a rough guide, curtains require the drop plus 15cm turnings by 2½ times the width, while festoons, the fullest of the blind styles, need only twice the width and twice the drop. Roman blinds only need the width and the drop plus turnings.

△ **Vertical emphasis**
Although vertical louvres are, generally speaking, associated with offices and commercial settings, they are well suited to domestic situations. Here, pale yellow vertical blinds co-ordinate perfectly with, and emphasize the vertical design of the striped vinyl wallpaper to create a very sophisticated feeling.

◁ **Co-ordinating rollers**
A sheer fabric with a lacy edge sets the theme for the dressing of this window. The bottom line of the patterned blind (which has been installed on top of the sheer fabric) has been cut to echo the scallops of the lace edging.

Meticulous attention to detail, through the use of co-ordinating wallpaper on the reveals around the top and sides of the window frame as well as on the walls, completes the scheme.

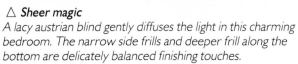

△ **Sheer magic**
A lacy austrian blind gently diffuses the light in this charming bedroom. The narrow side frills and deeper frill along the bottom are delicately balanced finishing touches.

△ **Simple but sophisticated**
The windows of this cream and white living room, with its unusual furniture and objets d'art, have been treated with great simplicity. The austrian blinds are made of a creamy, self-patterned fabric. The simple ruffled heading – created by threading a fixing pole through a casing a little below the top edge of the blind – has been precisely positioned so that it does not obscure the cornice.

◁ **A sense of spring**
This austrian blind, made out of an attractive and cheerful fabric, is like a breath of fresh air. The blind has a wide flounce of the same fabric, which is used again in the upholstery of the cushion covers. The large-scale floral design echoes the conservatory feeling of the cane furniture.

FESTOON BLINDS

Permanently ruched festoon blinds can be used on their own, in combination with curtains, or made up in sheer fabrics to replace net curtains.

Festoon blinds, rather like austrian blinds, are made up with a gathered heading, and have vertical tapes running down them to draw up the blind during the day. The difference is that festoon blinds contain up to twice as much fabric as austrian blinds. The vertical tapes ruche the fabric, giving deep and luxurious swags even when the blind is down. The style may be imitated for a pretty valance above a curtain.

The style does tend to cut out a certain amount of light even when the blinds are fully raised, so do not fit them if you want a lot of daylight. A frill along the lower edge, with optional piping included as well, gives a soft finish.

CHOOSE YOUR FABRICS

Because of the quantities involved, try to choose a fairly fine fabric. Silk, satin and moire are particularly effective, since the shiny surface shows off the folds as the light catches on them. You can also use plain or printed fabrics to co-ordinate with other furnishings – bedlinen, cushions and so on. Frills and piping can match or contrast with the main part of the blind.

The style is especially suitable for making up in sheer fabrics. If you intend to use the blinds in this fashion it is often possible to omit the cording completely since you may not want to draw up sheer festoon blinds during the day.

GATHERING UP THE FULLNESS

The top of the blind is usually made up with standard or pencil-pleated heading tape. The finer the fabric, the more fullness you should allow across the top: 1½–2 times the width is usually adequate. The blind is then hung from a track with curtain hooks.

More fullness is needed down the length of the blind to create the ruches: 1½–3 times is the usual amount. Again, the finer the fabric the greater the fullness required.

One problem you may have with this type of blind is that because it is made up in a fairly fine fabric it does not hang well and does not rise and fall smoothly. There are two ways of getting round this. One way is to stitch special festoon blind weights to the bottom of some or all of the vertical tapes – but particularly the outer ones – to keep the blind hanging straight. Another trick is to buy

A soft outlook
Gathered, piped and frilled along the lower edge, this festoon blind sits neatly inside the recess of an attic window. The subtle moire fabric shows off the folds of the blind.

a metal rod or wooden batten the same width as the finished blind, cover it in a remnant of matching fabric, and attach it to the back of the blind by stitching it to the bottom of the tapes. This helps to keep the tapes vertical and the lower edge level.

BRIGHT IDEA

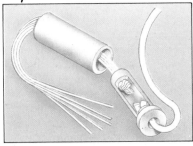

MEASURING UP

As with all forms of window dressing, start by fitting the track at the top of the window. It is advisable to fit the track to a batten so that it is held slightly away from the window, leaving room to fit screw eyes to carry the cords which will operate the blind. This style usually looks best hung from a simple track inside the recess – the top of the blind covers the track, so there is no need to use a fancy track. Measure up to find the finished size of the blind (the total width of the track and the drop of the blind from the top of the track to sill level).

CORD CONTROL

One of the problems with festoon, austrian or roman blinds is that you tend to get a tangle of cords at the side of the blind. A simple gadget converts the spaghetti of fine cords into a single cord, which is easier to wrap round the cleat to hold the blind in place.

It consists of a cylindrical plastic cord holder and a cover. After hanging the blind, cut off the cords at the side a couple of inches below the top of the blind. Thread them through the top of the cover, into the top of the cord holder and knot them together. Then thread a heavier length of cord into the bottom of the gadget, knot the end securely and then slip the cover over the top.

CALCULATING FABRIC QUANTITIES

Once you have measured to find the size of the finished blind, calculate how much fabric you will need. Check on the width of the fabric you plan to use before calculating exact quantities.

CHECK YOUR NEEDS

☐ Fabric for blind
☐ Curtain heading tape
☐ Lightweight standard tape and rings of festoon blind tape
☐ Cord to operate blind
☐ Contrast fabric and cord for piping (optional)

☐ Batten, track, hooks, screw eyes
☐ Cleat to hold cords
☐ Acorn (optional)
☐ Rod, batten or weights
☐ Tape measure
☐ Sewing thread, pins, needles
☐ Scissors
☐ Sewing machine

1 Width of fabric
The width of fabric to make up the blind is 1½–2 times the finished width, plus 2cm down each side for hems. If you have to join widths, allow 1.5cm for seams.

2 Length of fabric
Each of the widths of fabric needed to make up the blind should be 1½–3 times the finished length, plus 4cm seam allowance at the top and 1.5cm at the bottom where the frill is attached. (The finer the fabric, the greater the fullness required.) If you are using more than one width of fabric, multiply the drop by the appropriate number of widths to give the total amount of fabric for the main part of the blind.

3 Extra fabric
For a 10cm deep frill you will need a strip of fabric 12.5cm wide, and 1½ times the width of fabric calculated in Step 1. You will need another strip of fabric about 10cm wide and as long as the finished width of the blind if you are fitting a rod or batten to hold the lower edge of the blind level. If you want to insert piping between the frill and the blind, you will need a strip of fabric 4cm wide and as long as the finished width of the fabric calculated in Step 1. You will need the same length of fine piping cord.

4 Quantities of tape
Next, decide where to position the vertical tapes. They should be spaced about 25–40cm apart, with one positioned down each edge. Ensure that there is a tape covering any seams if you plan to join widths of fabric. Calculate how many tapes you will need, multiply by the total length of the blind calculated in Step 2, and then add a little extra for turnings. For the heading you will need a length of standard tape to match the width of the fabric as calculated in Step 1, plus 4cm for turnings.

5 Quantities of cord
Cord is needed to raise and lower the blind. Calculate 1½ times the length of the finished blind, add half the width of the finished blind and multiply by the number of vertical tapes. This allows the cord to hang about halfway down the window, even when the blind is down. (If you want the cord to hang lower down, increase the amount accordingly.)

MAKING UP THE BLIND

The blind itself is easy to make up. The piping (either matching or contrasting) is optional.

1 Join fabric widths
Cut out lengths of fabric. Join up strips of fabric to make up the frill, the optional piping, and the blind itself if necessary.

2 Prepare the piping △
Make up the piping: note that the fabric need not be bias-cut as it does not have to be eased round any corners. (See Creative DIY, page 32.)

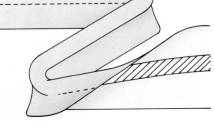

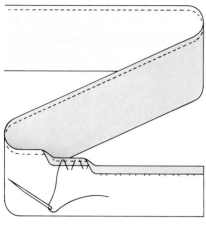
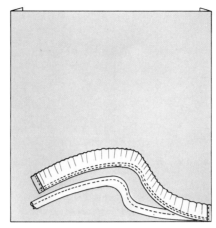
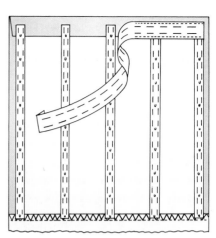

3 *Prepare the frill – rolled hem △*
The lower edge of the frill should be hemmed; either make a 5mm double hem or, for a more delicate finish, make a rolled hem by rolling the lower 1cm of the frill to the wrong side and then slipstitching in place. (A row of straight machine stitching along the edge of the fabric gives a firm edge, and so makes it easier to roll the hem.) Turn under a 1cm double hem at each end of the frill and then run two rows of gathering stitch along the unfinished edge.

4 *Attach the frill △*
Press a 2cm turning to the wrong side of the blind down each side edge. Draw up the gathering stitches of the frill so that it is the same width as the blind. With right side of blind facing you, lay the piping and then the frill across the lower edge so that right sides and raw edges are matching. Pin and tack in place, ensuring the fullness of the frill is evenly distributed. Stitch in place, taking 1.5cm seams, then zigzag stitch raw edges together and press upwards.

5 *Attach the tapes △*
Turn under 4cm along top edge of blind. Position vertical tapes evenly spaced across the blind, so that the side tapes cover the raw edges of the blind, and any vertical seams are covered. Pin and tack in place, turning under lower ends, then stitch close to the edge of each tape. Turn under 2cm at each end of heading tape, then pin, tack and stitch in place across the top of the curtain, so that the raw edges of the vertical tapes and the top turning of the blind are covered.

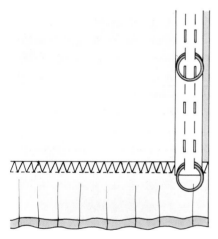
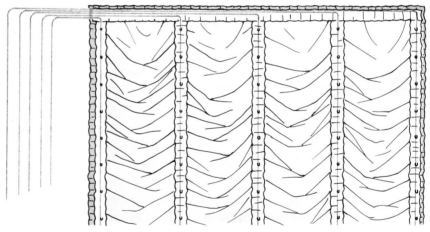

6 *Rings △*
If you have not used a specially designed festoon tape, slip split rings into the pockets in the vertical tapes at regular intervals.

7 *Draw up fullness*
Draw up the vertical tapes to give the appropriate drop to the blind, and draw up the heading tape to match the length of the curtain track.

8 *Add the cords △*
Decide which side the blind is to pull up. Cut lengths of cord so that they are long enough to run up each vertical tape, across the top of the blind and halfway down the side. Knot the cord to the bottom ring, and thread through the rings.

9 *Hang the blind ◁*
Fit a row of screw eyes to the lower edge of the batten which holds the track so that each one coincides with a vertical tape. Insert curtain hooks in the heading tape and hang the blind in place. Thread the cords through the screw eyes and bring them to one side of the blind. Knot together neatly, then plait them to keep them tidy. Fix a cleat to one side of the window.

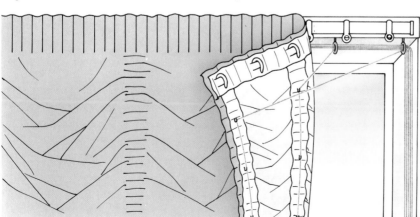

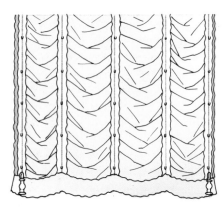

WEIGHTING THE BLIND

1 *Using festoon weights △*
Stitch a weight to the lower end of each of the side tapes (or thread on to split rings if used). If necessary, add extra weights across the width of the blind to ensure smooth working.

▽ Simply sumptuous
Curtains, a pelmet and a blind in co-ordinated fabrics give importance to a simple window. The curtains also co-ordinate with the wallpaper, which helps to give a more restful effect.

2 *Using a rod or batten △*
This has the advantage of both weighting the blind and holding it fully out to each side. You need a rod or batten the same width as the blind. Make up a tube of fabric slightly longer than the rod or batten, slip it inside the casing and stitch up the ends by hand. With the wrong side of the blind facing you, stitch the covered batten to the blind at the lower end of each tape, ensuring that the batten does not extend beyond the sides of the blind.

A cased heading is a neat alternative to a heading made in the usual way with heading tape. The top of the blind slips on to a rod or pole fixed across the top of the window. Allow a sufficient seam allowance at the top to make a casing to slip on to the rod or pole: you can use any type from a fine brass café rod to a substantial wooden pole. Lines of stitching above and below the rod ensure a crisp finish.

LINING WALLS WITH FABRIC

Fabric, tightly stretched over walls, creates an individual, luxurious finish — whatever your style of furnishings.

Fabric-covered walls add an opulent touch to any room. There is something about the feel and look of fabric which adds instant comfort and warmth. Tightly-stretched fabric is obviously more economical than fabric gathered on curtain rods and it also requires a lot less sewing.

One of the major benefits of using fabric to cover walls is that it can mask a multitude of lumps and bumps. Indeed, fabric wallcovering could become a positive economy measure if you managed to save on replastering a room.

There is a choice of techniques. You can buy the fabric and then have it professionally prepared and backed to hang like wallpaper. However, this is expensive and you have to be a skilled paper-hanger to hang the backed fabric without spreading paste on the right side of the fabric. Ready-backed fabrics are available, but again they are not cheap, and they are difficult to hang.

You can also have the fabric installed professionally, using specially designed tracks: the tracks grip the fabric, but it can still be taken down for cleaning.

For an effective finish, however, you can staple the fabric in place: the easiest way to do this is to fit battens to the wall first. With battens in place all round the area to be covered, you simply join widths of fabric to match the area, then turn under the edges and staple it all in place. For a crisp finish, you can wrap the edges of the fabric around very narrow battens, and then staple them in place. Other methods include making up a wooden framework, fixing the fabric to that and *then* fixing the wood to the wall; and covering panels of insulating board with fabric, and then fixing them to the wall.

Well-lined walls
Striped cotton gives a luxurious touch to what could be a rather austere room. The edges of the fabric have been finished with split bamboo.

SUITABLE FABRICS

Obviously, if money is no object you can choose luxurious fabrics like glazed chintz or rich velour, damask and watered silk. However, money usually *is* a problem, so you are likely to have to choose a more reasonably-priced fabric – calico, sheeting, or even curtain lining fabric, for example. It should be closely woven to prevent dust collecting behind it, and so it doesn't stretch out of shape. Striped patterns are very effective, adding height to a room and echoing 18th century elegance.

Trimmings and braids In most cases it is necessary to cover the edges of the fabric, where it is stapled in place. Use strips of the same fabric, made up like piping, or braid or other trimmings available by the metre. Bear in mind that this will add to the expense.

Extra warmth For a more luxurious effect, pad the walls with polyester wadding before putting up the fabric.

FIXED BATTEN METHOD

One of the most effective ways of fixing fabric to the wall is to staple it to battens fitted around the edge of the wall. The area within the battens can be lined with polyester wadding to provide additional warmth.

CHECK YOUR NEEDS

- ☐ Measuring tape, pencil and paper
- ☐ Fabric and scissors
- ☐ Wadding (optional)
- ☐ Staple gun
- ☐ Sewing machine and matching thread (for first two methods)
- ☐ Battens for fixing, 12.5×28mm or 4×22mm (plus saw, drill, screwdriver and wallplugs for larger sized battens)
- ☐ Dressmaker's chalk
- ☐ Braid or trimming and fabric glue
- ☐ Sturdy ladder

1 Measuring up ▷
Draw a sketch elevation of each wall. Mark in the exact measurements – both the overall measurements, from ceiling to skirting (the skirting boards remain exposed) and the dimensions of windows, doors, fireplaces and other features such as electric sockets. Divide the wall up into manageable rectangles and mark these areas on the sketch. Note down the measurements of each area, adding 10cm to each measurement to allow for the turnings.

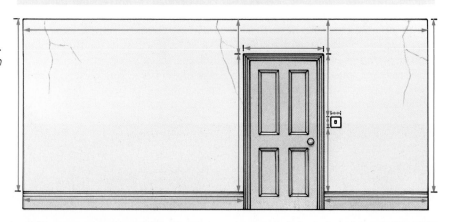

2 Calculate fabric amounts
Check the width of the fabric you intend to use. Calculate the number of widths you will need to make up the full width of each rectangle, rounding up to the nearest whole number. Multiply the number of widths by the height of the panel to give the amount of fabric required for each one. If there is a pattern repeat, make sure that the height of the panel is an exact number of pattern repeats and round it up if *necessary. Repeat for each panel and add together to give the total amount of fabric required. Repeat for the wadding, bearing in mind that the wadding will be fitted inside the battens, so you need slightly less.*

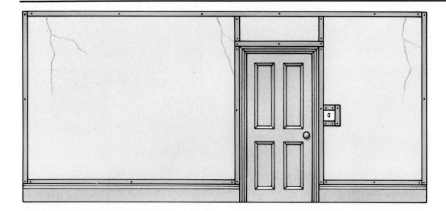

3 Fix the battens ◁
Fix 12.5×28mm battens firmly to the wall all round the edge of each 'panel' area, using wood screws and suitable wallplugs depending on how the walls are constructed.

At this stage, remember that you will have to re-fit light switches, electric sockets and wall lights. You must also fit battens for hanging pictures, since the fabric will stand 12.5mm (the thickness of the batten) away from the wall.

4 Begin fixing the wadding ▷
Decide which panel to line first. Check the height and width of the panel, measuring inside the battens. Cut sufficient lengths of wadding, the same size as the height of the panel, to cover the area. There is no need to join widths of wadding for larger panels. Starting on the left-hand side (if you are right-handed), climb up to ceiling level on a sturdy ladder. Hold up the first length of wadding flat against the wall, so that the top edge of the wadding meets the batten at the top of the wall. Staple the wadding to the wall across the top edge, keeping it taut without over-stretching it. (If the wall won't take staples, staple the wadding to the battens.) Position the staples about 10–15cm apart. Continue down side edges and across lower edge, trimming the wadding to fit as needed.

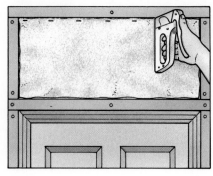

5 *Fix the rest of the wadding* ▷
Repeat the process for the remaining lengths of wadding, butting the edges together neatly. For the last length, staple the top edge in position, then staple the left-hand edge in place, butting up to the edge of the previous length; trim the right-hand edge so that it butts up to the batten before stapling it in place. Repeat for all the panels.

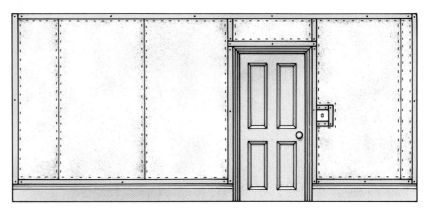

6 *Cut and join the fabric*
Cut sufficient lengths of fabric to make up the width of the first panel to be covered, allowing 10cm for turnings all round. Join the lengths down the selvedges, using flat seams, to make up a panel of fabric larger all round than the panel to be covered. Turn under and press a 10cm allowance along the top edge and down the left-hand edge. Don't turn under the right-hand edge and the lower edge yet. If the fabric has a pattern, make sure that this matches, not only across each panel, but from one panel to the next. For a perfect match, slip-tack the seams from the right side before stitching.

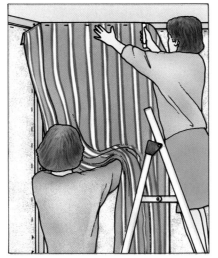

7 *Fix the fabric to the battens* ◁
This will be much easier if you have someone to hold the bulk of the fabric while you work. Start at the top left-hand corner of the panel to be covered. Staple the fabric to the top batten, positioning the staples so that they are within 1cm of the top of the wall, and so that they go through both layers of fabric before going into the batten. When the top edge is finished, check that it is hanging straight. Then staple the left-hand edge in the same way, keeping the fabric taut without stretching it out of shape.

8 *Fix the remaining edges*
Stretch the fabric across to the right-hand side of the panel and use dressmaker's chalk to mark a fold line to match the outer edge of the batten. Repeat for the lower edge, then fold under along the marked lines, and press with your fingers. Staple the remaining two edges as before, keeping the fabric taut without distorting it.

9 *Add the trimming* ▷
For a matching trimming, cut strips of fabric 4cm wide. Fold in half, right sides together and stitch down length, 1cm from raw edges. Trim seams and turn through to right side. Flatten out and glue to the walls over the staples, turning the ends of the tubes in for a neat finish. You can use braid or other trimming bought by the metre (right).

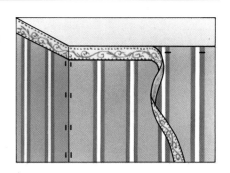

USING NARROW BATTENS
Narrow (4mm) battens can be used in different ways, depending on the effect required. Before deciding on this method, check that the walls are fairly sound, and that they are not too solid to take staples, particularly around windows, doors etc. There are sometimes very solid, concrete lintels above windows which are impossible to staple into. This method is suitable for rooms which can be easily divided into manageable areas. For larger areas, you can avoid any sewing by using the alternative to this method – see Step 6.

1 *Measure up*
Sketch out the walls as before, and mark in accurate dimensions. Add 5cm all round each of the panel areas. Calculate the length of fabric and the number of drops for each panel as before.

2 *Preparation*
Join fabric widths for each panel to be covered, allowing 5cm for turnings all round. Staple wadding in place, as described for the previous method, positioning the edges of the wadding about 1cm from the edge of the area.

3 *Start to fix the fabric* ◁
Cut a slim (4mm × 22mm) batten to the length of the area to be covered. Fold the top of the fabric over the batten, holding it in place with glue on long lengths. Get up the ladder and,

with someone supporting the bulk of the fabric and lifting it out of the way, staple the batten in place under the top layer of fabric, so that the turning of the fabric is sandwiched between the batten and the wall.

4 Fix lower edge of fabric
Stretch the fabric down over the batten, to give a crisp finish at the top. With the fabric stretched taut, turn under the lower edge of the fabric, and staple the folded edge close to the skirting. Finally, turn under and staple the sides.

5 Fit the trimmings
To finish the panels neatly, cover the staples with matching trimming or a contrasting braid, as described in Step 9 on page 41. You should not need as much braid with this method as with the fixed batten method, since the top edges will not need to be trimmed.

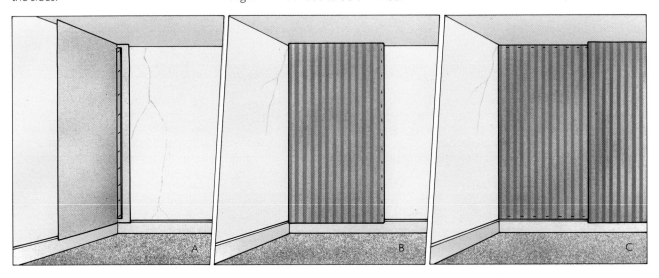

6 Alternative method △
To avoid joining widths of fabric, you can position the battens vertically instead. Cut lengths of fabric to run vertically down the walls. Wrap the left-hand selvedge over the first length of batten, cut to match the height of the area to be covered. Staple through the batten, so that the batten runs down the left-hand edge of the area to be covered, sandwiching the turning between the batten and the wall as before (A). Stretch the fabric to the right, so that there is a crisp edge down the batten. Turn the fabric under flush with the top and bottom of the wall to be covered. Staple the right-hand selvedge straight to the wall, so that the fabric is taut but not overstretched (B). Staple the top and bottom edges of the fabric straight to the wall. Take the next length of fabric, wrap it over the next length of batten, and staple through the batten and turning, so that the batten covers the staples and raw edge of the previous length of fabric (C). Finish by covering the last vertical row of staples and the staples at the top and bottom edges with trimming.

BRIGHT IDEA

Wood trim Rather than using fabric to trim the edges of the panels and cover the staples, you can use wooden beading to finish the job. Cut the beading to size, mitring the corners, and paint the wood or apply the required finish. Use fine panel pins, spaced every 15–20cm, to fix beading.

▷ **Blue mood**
Blue and white colour schemes have a particular freshness about them, adding a welcoming note to any room. The expertly lined walls give the room an added warmth. Fit battens for pictures before lining walls with fabric.

PUTTING PATTERNS ON FABRIC

Design and print your own furnishing fabrics quickly and inexpensively for a completely individual look.

Hand-painted T-shirts have been with us for some time; more unusual, perhaps, are hand-painted furnishing fabrics. Now, thanks to exciting developments in fabric dye and paint technology, quick, inexpensive designer-look fabrics can be yours. Bespoke fabrics like these can be colour-matched to walls and paintwork – you can even pick out patterns in an existing wallpaper or fabric and reproduce them on blinds, cushion covers, lampshades or deckchairs for a completely co-ordinated look.

KNOW YOUR FABRIC
Before you pick up a paint brush, it pays to do a little homework on suitable fabrics for painting and dyeing.

In general, natural fabrics are best: good quality cotton sheeting, jap (habu-tai) silk, fine linen, wool and lace are all suitable for painting but most man-made fibres, tweeds, corduroy, velvet and towelling are not – although the last three dye well. If in doubt test on a small piece, or write to the paint or dye manufacturer enclosing a cutting and a stamped envelope.

You can paint on light or dark coloured fabrics, though the colour of the fabric may affect the final colour. It is useful to know that if you paint on dark coloured fabric, adding some white fabric paint to any colour increases its opacity, helping the colour to show up better. In most cases, diluting fabric paints with water can make them difficult to work with; one paint, Pebeo, has a special diluter to combat this tendency.

Fabrics to be painted should also be free from manufacturer's dressing (in new fabrics), drip-dry and stain repellent finishes or starch – these all prevent colour from penetrating.

DYES & PAINTS
It's important to know the difference between a fabric dye and a paint. A dye such as Dylon's Cold Water Dye or Natural Dye actually penetrates the fibre while a fabric paint 'sits' on the fabric surface. However, some silk dyes are formulated to be 'painted' on; and some fabric paints also seem to penetrate fabrics better than others, giving a softer feeling finish.

There are several ranges of heat-setting fabric paints to choose from. You paint or draw the colour on and, after ironing, the pattern becomes washable and dry cleanable. Some ranges offer a wide range of fashion shades with a choice of opaque and transparent colours: opaque colour shows up on dark backgrounds; transparent colour is intended for white or very light backgrounds. Some paint ranges also include metallic and pearlized colours. Other fabric paints include wax pastels and felt-tip pens. All can be used on cotton, wool, linens and silk.

Shoe paints are specially formulated for painting leather and PVC but are also good for applying motifs to roller blinds and deckchairs.

For silk there are several ranges of special paints which have to be used with a barrier outliner that prevents colours 'bleeding' into each other.

INSPIRATION
Keep patterns simple. Unless you're an experienced artist, leave realistic cabbage roses and complicated trompe l'oeil effects until you gain more confidence. Concentrate instead on small geometric block prints and textured effects, action spattering and flicking. Or try stripes and dots at first before moving on to stencilled motifs, sponging and spray painting.

Plenty of abstract patterns and textures can be found in nature – tree bark, lichen-spotted walls and animal markings offer great pattern scope. Think of zebra and tiger stripes, leopard spots, crazy paving giraffe markings, tortoiseshell and snakeskin. It helps to have a few pictures of these animals around so you can study the patterns.

Leaves, shells and flowers also offer endless possibilities to the budding textile designer. However, don't feel you have to stick slavishly to natural colours. Professional designers enjoy turning colour upside down: pink leopard spots and green zebra stripes may make a more exciting fabric design.

If you are still unsure over colour combinations, remember that one-colour patterns in black or navy blue on a white background look effective.

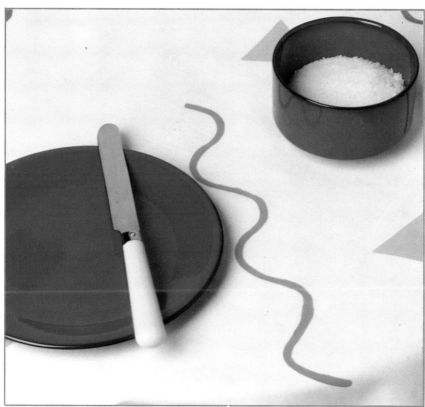

Abstract forms
Simple shapes – squiggles and triangles – in Dylon's Color Fun paints create a distinctive tablecloth. Repeat the pattern for blinds and cushions.

PREPARATION
Whatever method of applying pattern you intend to use, there are certain rules for making sure that the surface of the fabric you have chosen will take the colour successfully.

1 Clean the dry fabrics
All fabrics must be clean, dry and free of any manufacturer's finishes. Do not starch or use an ironing aid after washing. Press fabric to be painted, so that you start with a smooth surface.

2 Prepare made-up items
Slip a piece of polythene inside ready-made items such as cushion covers, duvets and pillowslips to prevent colour seeping through and marking the back.

3 Plan the pattern
Sketch the pattern on paper first. Then draw outlines very lightly in pencil, or use a special fabric felt pen – these are available in either broad or fine tips.

4 Practice makes perfect
With all the fabric painting techniques mentioned here you should try out the effects beforehand to check the consistency of the paint, so keep some spare fabric for this purpose.

STENCILLING
You can either cut shapes from stencil board with a sharp craft knife or buy them ready-made from good art shops. Draughtsmen's plastic letter templates from stationery shops may be useful. Pin out the fabric on padded softboard first.

1 Position the stencil ▷
Spray the back of the stencil with designer's low-tack adhesive before positioning it on the fabric – or hold it in place with masking tape. (Using spray adhesive on the back of a stencil gives better adhesion and there is less risk of the paint seeping under the stencil, giving blurred outlines.)

2 Apply the colour ▷
With the stencil held in place, apply the colour according to the type used. Pastels and pens are applied direct to the fabric. Some paints can be applied with a sponge, or you can use whichever type of paint brush gives the best results, depending on the paint and the fabric used. A combination of pens and paints may give the best effect.

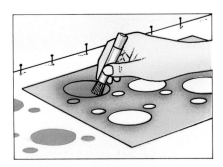

3 Apply subsequent colours
Always ensure one colour is dry (and iron it to fix it if necessary) before spraying the next stencil and applying the next colour.

SPONGING PATTERNS
This method can be used with stencils, or straight on to fabric to give a soft pattern. For best results, use a small sea sponge on cotton sheeting, muslin or fine silk. Line the backing board with white kitchen paper to absorb excess paint as you work.

1 Prepare the paint ▷
Tip a little of each of the different colours you plan to use on to a paper plate or old china dish. Dampen the sponge with clean water. Wring it out and then dip it into the first (palest) colour, and try it on a separate piece of fabric. If the effect is too heavy, make the sponge a little damper before dipping it in the paint, or apply less pressure.

2 Use the sponge ◁
Pad the sponge lightly over the fabric to be patterned, either to make a pattern of simple, repetitive shapes like trees or clouds, or simply to create a random textured effect. Work through from light to darker colours.
Check the kitchen paper from time to time. When it becomes wet and covered in paint, slip it out and replace it with clean, dry pieces.

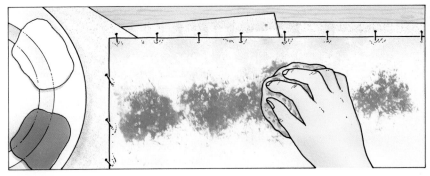

MAKING STRIPES

You can draw stripes freehand or use a ruler to mark the area, but they are much easier to produce if you mask out the areas which you don't want to be coloured.

1 Prepare the fabric
Pin out the fabric on a piece of softboard and stick masking tape over the areas you wish to leave unpainted. Pay particular attention to the edges of the tape.

2 Apply paint ▷
Apply the paint using a brush or a sponge. Allow the first colour to dry out before removing the masking tape and applying the next colour.

POTATO PRINTS

Although called potato prints, you can also use apples or carrots to achieve the same effect. Or try using blocks cut from wine bottle corks. The blocks have to be cut into simple shapes before they are used to apply the paint to the fabric.

You can use the technique to produce fairly regular patterns or to scatter shapes at random over the surface of the fabric. For regular patterns, you will get a neater effect if you use a pencil and ruler to mark the position of each row of shapes.

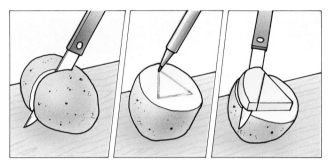

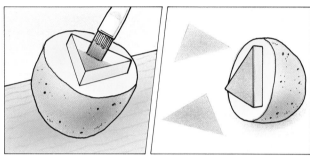

1 Cut the blocks △
Clean the potato and cut off one end to give a flat surface. Draw the outline of your pattern on the surface. Choose simple geometric motifs – a triangle, square, star or bar. Cut away the waste potato from around the edge of the motif to a depth of about 5mm.

2 Apply paint to the block △
Wipe the end of the potato with a dry cloth to remove excess water and starch. Load some fabric paint on to a soft brush and paint it over the end of the block, taking care not to overload the colour so that it oozes over the edge of the block when in use.

3 Print the shape on to the fabric △
Try the effect on a piece of scrap cloth first. Press the block on to the fabric, applying firm, even pressure, and lift it off immediately. You may be able to make several prints each time you load the block. Wipe clean and re-apply paint when necessary.

SPRAY PAINTING

Many types of paint can be applied using an ordinary plastic plant spray. For interesting effects you can apply the paint through an improvised stencil, such as a plastic doilie, coarse nylon lace or a draughtsmen's lettering template.

The main problem is getting the paint to the right consistency so that it does not clog the plant spray but still gives good colour on the fabric. Experiment with different paints on different fabrics until you get an interesting effect.

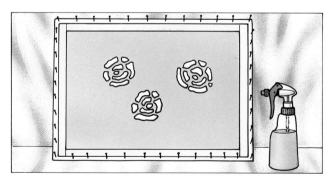

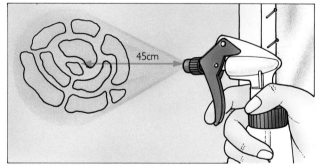

1 Prepare the area to be sprayed △
Pin out the fabric on a piece of softboard, with sheeting or kitchen paper behind it. Mask the surrounding area with sheets of polythene. Put the pinboard in an upright position. If you are using a stencil, hold it in place with low-tack spray adhesive or masking tape.

2 Prepare the paint
Mix paint in equal quantities with water and mix well. Put the mixture into a plant spray. For special, delicate effects on fine, tightly woven fabric such as silk, the paint can be thinned with up to 10 parts water.

3 Spray the paint △
Hold the plant spray upright and about 45cm away from the fabric. Create an even mist of paint by depressing the lever in short, sharp movements. Long, slow pressure will tend to produce heavy jets which cause drips and splashes. Keep the spray moving for an even effect.

PALETTE FLOWERS

This is a technique for producing bold, bright flowers, reminiscent of folk art and barge painting in particular. Use thick fabric paints, and lay on the paint with an ordinary kitchen spatula or a palette knife.

1 *Prepare the fabric and paint*
Set the fabric to be painted in an embroidery frame, or pin it over an old picture frame. Sketch out your design very lightly on to the fabric. Tip your chosen paint colours on to separate paper plates.

2 *Apply the paint* ▷
Dip the spatula into the paint and 'stroke' it on to the fabric. Repeat for each petal, turning the frame so that you can apply each stroke easily. Allow to dry before painting in the stalks. Use a felt pen for the stamens.

PAINTING ON SILK

You can achieve pretty effects with ordinary diluted fabric paints. There are also alcohol-based silk dyes in brilliant, translucent colours but some are difficult to apply and fixing the colour involves complicated steaming methods. However, the water-based Orient Ex- press paints from the Pebeo range and DEKA-silk paints both use a similar outlining method to prevent colours bleeding. Neither need steam fixing. The main pieces of equipment needed are a padded softboard and a picture frame the same size on which to stretch the area to be painted.

1 *Prepare the fabric*
Draw out the pattern you want to apply in felt tip on paper. Pin the paper on to padded softboard. Wash the silk; dry and press well. Pin it to the softboard, so that the drawing shows through.

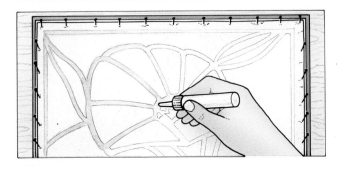

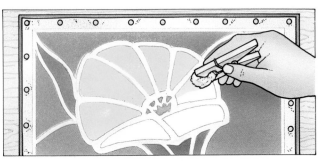

2 *Apply outlining fluid* △
Pierce the top of the cap of the applicator bottle containing the outlining fluid. Trace over the outline of the design, applying the applicator directly to the fabric. Leave to dry.

3 *Paint in the design* △
Remove silk from softboard and pin to the back of an old picture frame. Paint in the design with a paint brush – to paint large areas evenly, grip a swab of cotton wool with a clothes peg.

4 *Fix the paints*
The method of fixing the colours varies, so check the manufacturer's instructions.

BRIGHT IDEA

PENS AND PASTELS
The Pentel range of pastels can give a variety of effects ranging from naïve wax crayon children's drawings to a more sophisticated textured feeling. Leaf prints can also be achieved by rubbing the pastel on a dry but not crisp leaf, veined side up. Place the leaf waxed side down on the fabric, put a piece of white tissue paper on top and iron at medium.

Felt-tip fabric pens are good for filling in stencils – the colours are transparent and so can only be used on pale fabrics.

◁ *Sophisticated silk*
Simple but charming designs based on circles have been painted on to panels of silk to make up into large floor cushions.

PRINTING ON WALLS AND FABRIC

You can create your own wallpaper effects, and fabric to match, using simple block printing techniques.

Printing, like stencilling, is a method of producing your own pattern on walls and fabrics. There are no hard-and-fast rules for the technique: one designer, Cressida Bell, simply took a sponge and cut it in the shape of a leaf, dipped it in paint and dabbed it all over the bedroom wall. Confidence is a prerequisite if you are considering attempting this method of decorating.

PAINTS AND SURFACES

Whatever design and finished effect you want to achieve, the most important thing is to start with a properly prepared surface, which is ready to take the appropriate paint.

Walls must be in reasonable condition: previously painted walls are ideal, as long as there are no signs of the paint flaking or peeling. If the surface is loose, scrape off any peeling paint, and brush down with a wire brush. Apply a coat of stabilizing solution, and then a couple of coats of emulsion in your chosen background colour.

The overall effect of the printing technique described here is rather rustic, so a paint effect such as colour washing is particularly appropriate as a background.

You can use emulsion paints, if you can find appropriate colours, but you will get a more defined effect with powder paints, which are available in stronger colours and can be mixed to a slightly thicker consistency than emulsion. Another alternative is to use artist's acrylic paints, which are water-based, strongly coloured, and produce a more permanent finish than powder paint.

Wood Woodwork and pieces of furniture can also be decorated by this technique. Again, the surface must be sound. Such surfaces are normally finished with oil-based varnish or paint. Matt or eggshell finishes are more appropriate than high gloss ones.

For printing, use artist's oil colours, or ordinary gloss or eggshell paint, tinted with universal stainers or artist's oil colours. You can also use transparent, oil-based glaze, tinted with stainers or

In the print

Simple squares and traditional fleurs de lys *have been used to decorate these plain glazed cottons. And acrylic artist's colours, painted on to ivy leaves, make a rustic border to decorate plain walls.*

oil colours, and white eggshell paint to make it less translucent. However, the reason for using such a glaze with other paint effects is to slow down drying times, which is not desirable with printing.

Fabrics When printing on fabrics always ensure that they are clean and dry before you start. Any dressing which has been applied to new fabrics must be completely removed – which may also mean that the fabric loses some of its body. To replace the crispness, starch the fabric after printing.

Use a versatile fabric paint, such as Dylon's Color Fun paints. Most fabric paints are water based, so they can be thinned down easily if necessary. They are then fixed by pressing with a hot iron (follow the manufacturer's instructions).

TOOLS AND EQUIPMENT

As with so many paint techniques, improvisation is the catchword. An evenly textured sponge can produce good prints and fine textured, cosmetic and baby sponges are particularly effective. Leaves (collected in the summer when they are strong but not crisp) also give interesting effects. You could even use potatoes or apples to create an innovative design. Another alternative is to use a stubby pencil brush, dabbing it on the wall to make groups of spots to form a pattern.

A plain wallpaper border, available from craft shops for stencilling, makes it easy to print border patterns for use on walls.

You will also need a palette of some kind: an old dinner plate is probably the best choice. You can put a blob of paint at the edge of the plate and spread some over the flat surface to dip the printing block into.

Do not expect to achieve smooth, even prints: the charm of this method of decorating is that the result is rustic and slightly blotchy – if you want a polished result you are better off decorating with wallpaper.

PLANNING THE DESIGN

The design you choose depends on the surface you are painting, the type of room you are decorating, the material you are using to print with and the type of paint you choose. Plan out the design roughly before you start: the prints need not be spaced evenly, but some guidelines will help to prevent bunching. The examples shown here are marked on walls, but could equally well apply to fabrics.

CHECK YOUR NEEDS

☐ Chalk, rule and tape measure (for marking out walls)
☐ Plain wallpaper border, to make printing border designs easier
☐ Dressmaker's chalk (for marking out fabrics)
☐ Frame to stretch fabrics over
☐ Appropriate paint (emulsion, powder paint, Color Fun fabric paint, oil-based paint, etc)
☐ Sponge, rubber or leaf to make prints with
☐ Craft knife to cut out shape if necessary
☐ Palette
☐ Brush to apply paint to block or leaf if necessary
☐ Iron to set fabric paints

1 *All-over patterns* ▷
For an all-over pattern, mark a grid on the wall using chalk and a metre rule. First measure the wall and decide on a suitable spacing for the motifs, then mark a grid on the wall to suit the size of the motif: you could position one large motif in each square, or, if you are using a smaller motif, set a certain number of images in each square.

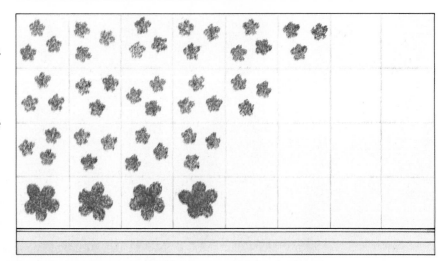

2 *Diagonal patterns* ◁
Mark out the grid diagonally if you want motifs to form a diamond pattern. You can either space the motifs in the grid as before, or give the impression of a trellis by positioning the motifs close to the marked diagonals.

3 Freestyle designs ▷
In some situations, you may want to group motifs around an architectural feature – a fireplace, window or doorway, for example. In this case, simply sketch a line to indicate the area where the motifs should be concentrated, just allowing one or two motifs to stray outside the marked line for a casual effect.

4 Patterns on fabrics
It is easier to apply patterns to fabrics before making up items (such as curtains, tablecloths or loose covers). Measure up carefully and mark where the seam lines are to be, then cut out, leaving a larger seam allowance than normal. Mark out the pattern area with dressmaker's chalk, which can be brushed off (or washed out if necessary) once the fabric paint has been fixed (by pressing).

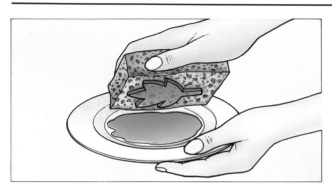

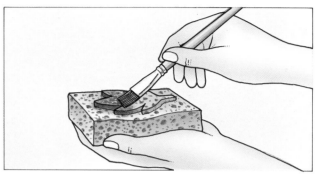

PRINTING TECHNIQUES

There are two main methods of applying the paint to the printing block. The one you choose depends on the type of paint you are using and the material the printing block is made of.

1 Paint palette △
This method is very simple. Spread a shallow pool of paint over a palette (an old, flat-bottomed dinner plate is ideal). Dip the printing block into the paint, ensuring it is evenly covered, then stamp it on to the wall. You may need to re-load the block each time, although most types of sponge will only need re-loading after several prints.

2 Brushing it on △
You can also apply the paint to the block with a brush. Try to avoid letting the paint run on to the surfaces which do not form part of the print. This is easiest with a soft artist's brush.

MAKING DESIGNS

Below are a number of suggestions for designs for various situations.

1 Leaves around a doorway ▷
This design uses sycamore leaves to print patterns on a wall. The paint is artist's acrylic, thinned with water. Arrange the prints within an area sketched on the wall. For best results, choose natural leaf greens and autumnal hues. A little variation in colour from leaf to leaf will enhance the effect. Put a blob of paint on the palette. Dip a thick, soft, artist's brush in water, and then into the paint. Spread the paint over the top of the leaf and then apply the leaf to the wall.

2 Sponge fans ▷
An ordinary, rectangular car sponge can be used to create interesting effects on walls. Mix the paint you wish to use to a creamy consistency, so that it soaks into the sponge but does not run down the surface when dabbed on. Mark chalk guidelines on to the wall. For a graduated effect, apply one colour and then fill in with a second, toning shade.

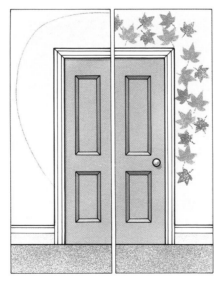

3 Rings of spots △
Chunky pieces of furniture look less bulky if they are painted in pale colours. Prepare them by removing any existing finish, then apply knotting, undercoat and a top coat of oil-based eggshell paint. To create the decorative, spotted effect shown here, use chalk to mark circles on the furniture (use a dinner plate as a template). When you are happy with the spacing of the circles, fill each one in with spots made with a stencil brush, using oil-based paint in a slightly deeper tone than the background colour.

4 Fabric patterns ▷
Design patterns for fabrics to co-ordinate with patterns you have used on the walls. Sponges make the best prints, but be careful not to overload the sponge or the colour will bleed into the fabric. Always stretch the fabric over a frame before starting, and lay a pad of another fabric behind.

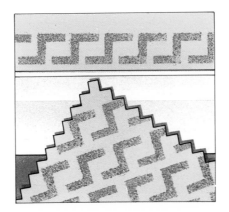

5 Lampshades
You can also apply patterns to ready-made lampshades: there is no need to fix the paint with an iron in this situation, as you will not need to wash the lampshade. Because of their shape, any geometric pattern (vertical stripes or a trellis, for example) must be very carefully planned so that it tapers to match the shade. Trust your eye when planning such designs, rather than taking accurate measurements and making involved calculations.

COMPLETE CO-ORDINATION

Co-ordinating patterns on fabrics, walls and other accessories give an extra dimension to painting your own patterns. However, you must choose the paints carefully: you may be able to find a perfect colour to print your design on the wall, but finding a fabric paint in a matching colour is a different matter.

You can take the idea further, and repeat the design on china and glass using suitable paints. Again, you may have problems matching colours, so check out all the colour ranges before you start. Using a different range of paints or altering your colour choice slightly may save mixing paints. If you do have to mix colours, make up enough in one go to cover the whole area without having to prepare a second batch.

You need not use identical motifs for all the surfaces in the same room. It is often more effective to vary the scale or the spacing of the motif, to give a different density of pattern which suits the size and shape of the different surfaces better.

Border line
Emphasize the height of the ceiling with a row of leaf prints cut from a sponge and positioned around the top of the wall.

Up the wall
Create an all-over pattern with a stylized flower motif, printed over a colour washed wall.

Floral tribute
The same stylized flower has been used in a smaller scale on a plain lampshade.

Nature trail
Use an oil-based paint to print motifs on a wooden chest. An extra coat of matt polyurethane varnish will protect the finish.

Curtain call
Plain cotton or linen curtains can become part of the scheme with vertical borders, echoing the border around the ceiling.

Easy does it
Give a plain loose cover an extra lift with printed motifs along the flat, gussetted parts. The two motifs are combined to decorate the silk cushion.

DESIGNS ON WALLS

Enliven dull rooms with decorative walls and experiment with bold abstracts or witty trompe l'oeil finishes.

With a little imagination, careful planning and an accurate assessment of your artistic abilities, a number of paint finishes are within your reach. It's not essential to be as talented as Michelangelo, as long as you recognize your limitations before you start. Don't embark on an ambitious project which involves complicated details plus a fine eye for freehand drawing if it's your first attempt.

Sophisticated trompe l'oeil excepted, murals and strong abstract designs are probably best applied to rooms where there are few interesting features with which they may compete. Bathrooms, halls and children's rooms are popular choices, the last often decorated with cartoon characters. Being two-dimensional, they are relatively simple to execute, however humble your artistic talents. Strong abstract or graphic designs will cheer up a hall or enliven even the dullest bathroom. They can also pull a room scheme together or co-ordinate with it.

Your choice of oil- or water-based paints is governed by the effect you want to achieve, and whether the paint has to dry quickly. If you don't want to mix your own colours, have a good look at what ready-mixed paints are available, before making a final decision about your design.

△ **Elevations**
The mural in this bathroom has been stencilled, and relies on a mixture of ready-made and specially-designed stencils. The images are designed to fill the entire wall space between two borders, one just below the ceiling, and the other just above the tiled splashback. The design of the mural is deceptively simple, and the soft colours have been applied to indicate shadows and give a three-dimensional feeling.

▷ **Bright relief**
Pale grey sanitaryware and strong earthy tones create a glowing bathroom. A relief wallcovering provides a textured surface so that the rich terracotta does not overwhelm the room as it might do if used as flat colour. The checkered 'splashback' around the bath is not in fact tiles, but simply painted squares of the same two colours used elsewhere in the room to highlight the design of the wallcovering. The castellated finish along the bottom of the roller blind echoes the illusion of checkered tiles.

△ Dutch influence

An architrave has been fixed to a plain wall, and trompe l'oeil on a panel gives the illusion of a room seen through a doorway, in the manner of a Vermeer painting. The perspective must be right if trompe l'oeil, which translates literally to mean 'something that deceives the eye', is to succeed. Notice how the skirting has been removed to make the illusion more convincing.

△ Radiator camouflage

The first stage of this cunning scheme was to prepare the surfaces of the walls and radiator. Having planned the design, it was then transferred to the wall surface by masking off the stripes, and the blue-green paint was sponged between the guidelines. Once the paint had dried, the masking tape was removed and the painted stripe masked over. Pink, apricot and yellow were then applied with rough brush strokes over the rest of the walls and radiator. To complete the scheme, the skirting was ragged in the same sea-green.

◁ Check it up

Before undertaking such a bold check design, plan it out carefully to make sure that the lines won't dissect one another unhappily. Once the design has been planned, mark it up carefully, taking care to keep the verticals upright, and the horizontals straight by using a spirit level and a plumbline. The vertical stripes were painted before the horizontal stripes, and each stripe was painted between two parallel lines of masking tape. Allow the paint to dry thoroughly before removing the masks to prevent smudging.

SPECIAL EFFECT PAINT FINISHES

Subtle, serious outrageous or just plain fun, paint finishes can enliven or transform your home.

The term 'special effect paint finishes' covers many techniques and materials, and differing combinations of the two. There are no strict rules: the project you have in mind, your confidence in your own abilities and the result you want to see are the governing factors.

Complicated paint effects are not necessarily the most effective – especially if it's your first attempt. Start with simple techniques like ragging and sponging, before trying marbling and tortoiseshelling. The larger the area to be decorated, and the faster drying the glaze or paint, the more difficult it is to make the job look professional. If you are unsure of yourself, save complicated finishes for furniture and use simpler paint effects on walls. Have fun experimenting with different surfaces and finishes.

Dark colours bring special effect paint finishes into a league of their own. Broken or distressed finishes mean you can use rich and sumptuous colours without making a room feel oppressive or overwhelming. Because the dark colour is contained in a translucent glaze applied over a pale base, it gives an impression of 'movement' quite different from a wall of solid colour – and a lot easier to live with.

△ *Check it up*
A plain doorway has been given a new identity and a renewed sense of purpose. Strong, painted graphics (achieved with the aid of masking tape) link the architrave to the black and white checked table, a black triangle on the wall, an unusual vase and a tropical plant in the room beyond.

◁ *A grand entrance*
The walls and doors in this hall have been panelled with applied mouldings, before being decorated. A creamy yellow paint, applied to walls, doors and mouldings, has been sponged over with a darker yellow/old gold colour. Sponging is a simple paint finish, but need not look amateurish – on the contrary, this hall is both refined and sophisticated.

◁ *Hepplewhite and green*
This Hepplewhite-style chair has been stripped, bleached and stencilled. The paint technique is simplicity itself, and the end result is light and fresh. Thin, dark green lines add definition to the frame of the chair, while the soft green of the painted motifs has been matched to the seat and the braid. A steady hand and an eye for detail are the main skills required in the execution of this decorative treatment.

△ *Find your niche*
This witty trompe l'oeil of a wash-hand basin is part fact, part fantasy. The niche is real, the windows and the view are not; the towels are, but the tiles are not; the toilet bags and soap are, but the basin itself is pure fiction.

Trompe l'oeil requires some planning, and once you've established a light source, you must stick with it, as shadows are all important in visual trickery. Try to find an area with limited viewpoints for your mural – such as the end of a corridor – as the perspective is much more convincing if viewed from the intended angle.

◁ *Country comes to town*
Oak furniture, quarry tiles and ladderback chairs with rush seats bring a rustic atmosphere to this large town kitchen. The window frame, shutters and kitchen units have been roughly dragged in a dark blue-green over a lighter base. The depth of colour does not overwhelm this dining area, nor does it make the room too dark, which it might well have done had flat emulsion been used. This three-dimensional quality of special paint finishes is worth bearing in mind if you like dark colours. The same qualities are visible in the sponged terracotta-coloured panels on the shutters.

BEAUTIFULLY DRESSED BEDS

A well-presented bed is an important decorative element in creating an attractive bedroom.

The bed is usually the largest single piece of furniture in a bedroom, so the bed cover, bedhead and, to a slightly lesser extent, the bedlinen all have to complement the colours and fabrics used in the room.

In a mainly flowery scheme you could pick out one or two plain colours for the bed. Checks can work very well with flowers; for instance, bedcoverings and linen in different-sized checks in the flower colours.

In a plainer room you could make the bed the centre of interest by concentrating pattern in this area.

The style of bed treatment helps to create the mood of the room. A fitted bedspread with contrast piping and similar cushions will accentuate the tailored feel of built-in units.

For a softer, more romantic look, try a squashy duvet and piles of pillows in pastel colours; or fine white cotton bedcover and pillows edged with lace, or frilled and trimmed with ribbon.

For a real touch of luxury, choose a draped bed: a corona, half-tester, or four-poster effect. A simple four-poster look can be created in a small room by pushing the bed close up to the window. The curtains on that side do double duty for bed and window and the other curtains are ceiling-mounted. This is very effective if the bed fills the whole space across the window.

Flower draped
A romantic look for a tiny room where the window curtains double as bed drapes. Pale mint green accents this mainly flowery scheme.

◁ **Victorian mood**
The delicate lines of an old white-painted iron and brass bedstead need showing off, not disguising with heavy fabrics and pattern. The beauty of this one is enhanced by hanging it with old fine lace panels in sympathetic designs.

The bedcover has a crunchier texture. It is an old knitted one whose charm is not lessened by the odd sign of wear.

Cushions are covered in a variety of different types of lace with an embroidered one for contrast.

◁ Classic elegance

A plain white shell allows scope for a variety of treatments. Here the room takes its colour scheme and elegant mood from the bed. The same patterned fabric used for the formal corona appears on the bedhead, valance and curtains, with the dominant cyclamen colour as accent.

The frill detail at the top of the corona is picked up on the top of the curtains. The track is covered by plain white pelmets which 'disappear' into the ceiling. The motif of the fabric – wide knotted ribbons – is echoed by the extravagantly tied bows on the curtains.

Textural interest and a change of pace is provided by a heavy crocheted and knitted bedcover.

▽ Tailored black and white

Textures and streamlining are the keynotes in this dramatic room. Shiny black lacquer furniture contrasts with a white quilted satin bedcover and relief-patterned walls. The scheme is strongly influenced by the 1930s – the curving lines of the suite, the motif of the wallcovering, the wall lights and ornaments.

BRIGHT IDEA

LACY CUSHIONS

To complement a Victorian room scheme or soften a modern one add a few broderie anglaise or lace-trimmed cushions.

It is still possible to buy inexpensive scraps of old lace which can be joined to make cushions.

Remnants of silk, too small for any other purpose, can be used for cushions. Alternatively, cut out good sections from old embroidered or damask tablecloths and edge them with cotton lace.

QUILTED THROWOVER

Quilting will turn a simple throwover cover into a luxurious comforter.

Decide on the size of bedspread and add 15% to the width and length to allow for 'shrinkage' caused by stitching the quilting.

You will need the same amount of fabric for the top and reverse side and an equal area of medium- or heavyweight polyester wadding for the filling; plus enough fabric to bind the edges.

Joining the fabric Join widths of fabric with 1.5cm flat seams to make up required size. Press seams open.

▽ *White-on-white*
A plain spread is given textural interest with a simple quilted pattern, a deep frill and pale grey ribbon insertions.

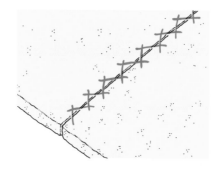

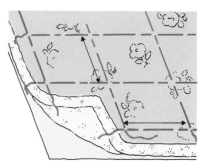

1. Preparation

You will almost certainly need more than one width of wadding. Lay two pieces side by side with edges butting (do not overlap them). Join with large herringbone stitches.

Lay the top fabric on a flat surface with right side up and use tailor's chalk to draw guidelines for the quilting (a grid or diamond pattern is the most straightforward choice). Make sure the lines are absolutely parallel.

2. Joining the layers

Lay the reverse side fabric out flat, wrong side up, and place wadding on top. Lay top fabric over the wadding, right side up. Tack all three layers together; tack all round the edge and in lines across the length and width of fabric about 15cm apart. Machine-stitch the lines of quilting along the chalked guide lines; stitch all the vertical lines, then all the horizontal ones.

BED CANOPIES AND DRAPES

Turn your bedroom into a special retreat with one of these ideas for creating a focal point above the head of the bed.

The original four-poster beds served a practical purpose – the curtains were of heavy woven fabrics, to draw round the bed and keep out the draughts at night. Now, however, bed drapes and canopies are fitted purely for decoration – and very luxurious decoration at that.

There are many different ways of fitting and fixing curtains at the head of a bed; for example, you could fit a simple curtain track at ceiling height for draping plain, unlined curtains; you can fit fine tracks to the ceiling all round the bed and hang diaphanous sheers for a mosquito net effect; you can fix wooden curtain poles to the ceiling at the head and foot of the bed and drape a length of fabric over them; or you can create a coronet effect by fitting a semi-circular board above the head of the bed, with drapes fitted to it. The only real restriction is finding suitable fixing points; heavier styles must be fitted to the joists, or to battens fitted between joists.

CHOOSE YOUR FABRICS
Your choice of fabric depends on the other furnishings in the room and the effect you want; you could use metre upon metre of butter muslin, tied and draped for an extravagant effect; or you could make stark, flat curtains from mattress ticking for an unfussy effect. In most situations, however, fabrics to match the curtains at the windows, or sheeting to match the bedding, are most appropriate. For many styles, including those shown here, the lining is on display as much as the main fabric. In this case, it is a nice idea to choose a broken colour pattern for the lining to tone with the main fabric used.

Bedrooms are one area of the home where it is fun to go to town with metres of fabric, frills, flounces and contrast piping, so consider fabrics for these finishing touches as well. Try to ensure that the fabrics used for canopies and drapes tie in with those used elsewhere in the room.

FIXTURES AND FITTINGS
Once you have decided on a particular style, you have to fix the necessary hardware to hold the curtains in place. Fixing the curtain tracks to the wall above the bed should be relatively straightforward; if the wall is solid, tracks or poles can be fixed using standard wall plugs and screws. If the wall is hollow, the tracks should be fitted to the wooden studs in the wall which are 30-40cm apart.

If you are fitting tracks or poles to the ceiling, again, you should fit them to the wooden joists supporting the ceiling, just like fitting to a stud wall. If there is not a joist exactly where you want to fit a track you have two choices: the simplest is to adjust the design and position of the tracks slightly so they do coincide with the positions of the joists. Alternatively, in a top floor bedroom where you have access to the loft above, you could set an extra noggin in between the joists (see diagram).

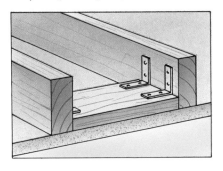

For coronets, there are various ways of fixing the drapes above the bed. The simplest method, as long as the drapes hide the fixings, is to cut a semicircle of chipboard, paint it or cover it with fabric, and fix it to the wall with metal brackets. Then you can fit screw eyes to the side and lower edge of the board, staple the fabric in place using a heavy-duty staple gun, or hold the drapes in place with Velcro as long as they are not too heavy.

TAPES AND CASINGS
The two main methods of gathering and fitting the canopies and drapes described here are with tapes or casings. Curtain heading tapes give a neatly gathered effect at the head of a curtain, and vertical blind tapes can be used for vertical gathers. Calculate the lengths of tape needed in the same way as for curtains and austrian blinds.

In some situations you can make a cased heading and slot the top of the canopy on to a pole, creating gathers if you want a ruched effect, or using a piece of fabric the same width as the pole for a simpler effect.

Crowning glory
Turn a quite ordinary bedroom into somewhere special with a coronet-style canopy and matching drapes. For extra effect, the coronet and curtains match the valance and curtains at the windows.

CORONET AND DRAPE

This style, pictured on page 59, involves a ruched and frilled coronet, topping a lined curtain which has a matching frill and is held to either side of the bed with a decorative brass knob or hold-back.

pictured on page 59

CHECK YOUR NEEDS

- ☐ Main fabric, and contrast fabric for frills, binding and lining as needed
- ☐ Sewing thread
- ☐ Heading tape and vertical blind tape, as needed
- ☐ Appropriate hardware
- ☐ Drill and screwdriver for fixing
- ☐ Sewing machine
- ☐ Dressmaker's chalk
- ☐ Tape measure
- ☐ Scissors
- ☐ Pins and needles

1 Fit the hardware ▷
Decide how to hang the two layers of fabric at the head of the bed; in the example here, both the coronet (or valance) section and the drape (or curtain) have pencil-pleated gathered headings; a semicircle of chipboard, painted to match the decor, is fitted to the ceiling. A series of screw eyes is fitted all round the lower edge, about 3cm apart, to hold the drape. Another set of screw eyes is fitted round the curved outer edge of the chipboard, spaced 3cm apart, to hold the coronet. (You could use Velcro instead of the outer screw eyes.)

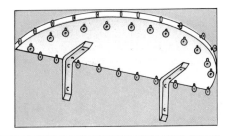

2 Measure up
Measure all round the semicircle, where the lower screw eyes are fixed, to find the finished width of the drape. Measure the outer curved edge for the finished width of the coronet. Drape the tape measure from the semicircle over the hold-back position to the floor, to judge the length of the drape.

3 Fabric for the drape
For a drape with a pencil-pleated heading, multiply the first measurement in previous step by three. Check that this will be wide enough to reach comfortably from one side of the bed to the other, with a little extra fullness. Add 1.5cm for any seams needed, and 2cm down each side edge. For the length, add a 4cm allowance for the heading and a 2cm allowance for hems. (Note that here the curtain has a straight hem, which will cascade on the floor by the bed. You could shape the hem if you prefer.) You will need the same amount of fabric for lining. For the frill, you will need two 12cm-wide strips, 1½ times the finished length.

4 Fabric for the coronet
For the coronet section, multiply the distance around the semicircle by three for the width of fabric required, adding 2cm at each side for turnings. Decide on a suitable depth; about a sixth of the distance from the fixing point to the level of the bed gives pleasing proportions. The length of fabric required will be the finished length of the coronet plus 4cm for the heading and a 2cm turning allowance for hem. For the frill you will need a 12cm-wide strip, 1½ times the width of the fabric for the coronet. You will need the same amount of fabric for lining.

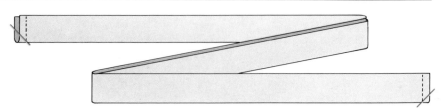

5 Make up the frills △
Cut sufficient 12cm-wide strips of fabric to make up two frills, each 1½ times the length of the curtain. Fold in half, right sides facing, along length, and stitch across short ends, taking 1cm seams. Clip corners and trim seam allowances; turn right sides out and press.

6 Gather frills
Run two lines of gathering threads through both layers of the long, unfinished edge of the frill and draw up fullness to match the finished length of the curtain.

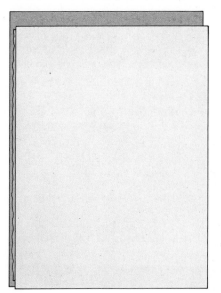

7 Make up the curtain ◁
Cut fabric and lining fabric to the measurements calculated in Step 2, joining widths if necessary. Trim 4cm from the top edge of the lining and position lining on top of main fabric, right sides facing, with remaining three edges matching. Position frill between the two layers of fabric aligning top edge of frill with top of lining (4cm from top of curtain). The frill should end 2cm from lower edge of curtain. Pin, and tack.

8 Stitch frill and curtain ▷
Stitch down sides and across lower edge of curtain, taking 2cm seams. Trim seam allowance, clip corners and turn curtain right side out and press.

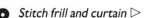
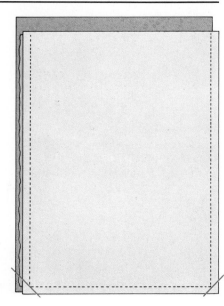

9 *Attach heading tape* ▷
Turn top 4cm of curtain fabric over lining and pin in place. Position pencil pleated tape across top of curtain, and turn under ends. Pin, tack and stitch tape in place.

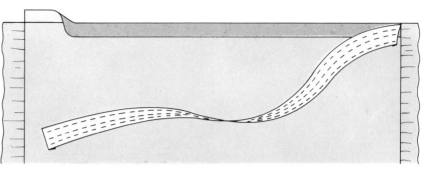

10 Draw up cords
Draw up cords through heading tape and insert hooks into pockets ready to hang round coronet board.

11 *Make up coronet* ◁
Make up a single frill to fit the lower edge of the coronet and make up the coronet in the same way as curtain, inserting frill along the lower edge rather than down the side edges.

12 *Create the flounces* ▷
To create a ruched effect you can either fit vertical blind tapes to the back of the coronet, in the same way as an austrian blind, or gather the canopy by hand with a double row of gathering stitches at each of five or six gathering points. (Don't forget that you must gather the curtain at each side, as well as at three or four points around the coronet.)

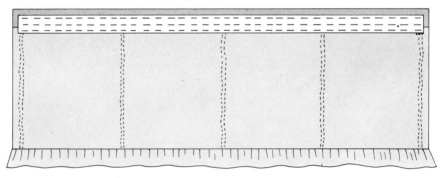

13 *Hang the drapes*
Hang the curtain and coronet to check the effect. Hold the sides of the curtain out and decide where to fit the hold-backs. Mark the position of the hold-back and the finished length of the buttonhole with dressmaker's chalk.

14 *Bind the buttonholes* ▷
Take down the drape and make lines of tacking stitches at each end of the buttonhole and above and below the position of the slit, 1cm away from it. Cut in diagonally from each corner, and along the line of the slit as shown (A). Cut two strips of fabric, 2cm wide and 1cm longer than the finished buttonhole. Fold them in half along their length, wrong sides together. Pin and tack them to the curtain, with raw edges to centre of buttonhole. Stitch in place along marked lines above and below buttonhole, ending stitching in line with the end of the slit (B). Turn fabric strips through to the lined side of the curtain (C). Fold back the frilled edge of the curtain, keeping the binding strips flat. There will be a small triangular flap at the end of the slit; tack and stitch the triangle to the binding strips (D). Repeat for the other end of the buttonhole.

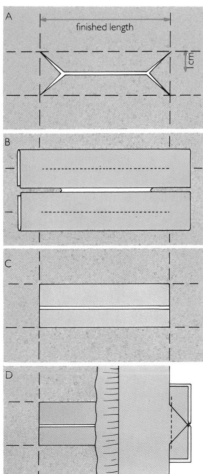

SINGLE BED CANOPY

This type of canopy, shown hung over a single bed overleaf, could equally well be used at the head of a double bed and draped to either side. Instead of being held in place by the head and foot of the bed, you could use tiebacks or hold-backs. The canopy is slotted on to a short pole (40cm or so) which is fitted to the wall by means of a purpose-designed bracket so that it sticks out at right angles. You can adapt the arrangement and make a more secure fixing by fitting the pole close to ceiling level, and using a bracket fitted to the ceiling to hold the protruding end in position.

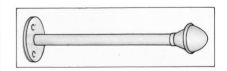

1 *Fit the hardware* △
There are a number of purpose-designed poles available to fit above a bed; a bracket is fitted to the wall and the pole slots or screws into that. Decide where to fit the pole, making sure there is a wooden stud in the wall at the appropriate point if the wall is not solid.

2 Measure up ▽
Measure the length of the canopy, from floor level at one end of the bed, up and over the pole and down to floor level at the other end of the bed.

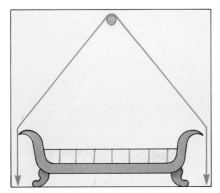

3 Calculate fabric amounts
In most cases the canopy can be made from a single width of fabric; any more might be too heavy for the pole. The length should be the measured length from Step 1, plus 2cm at each end for seam allowance, plus an extra 15-20cm for ease, to allow for the stitching around the pole, and for a slight drape down the length of the canopy. You will need the same amount of main fabric and lining, plus sufficient fabric to bind the 'leading' or front edge of the canopy. (This may be ready-made 2.5cm wide bias binding or, for a more luxurious effect, use plain fabric to cut your own bias strips.)

4 Make up the canopy △
Cut out the fabric and lay the lining fabric on top of the main fabric, right sides facing and raw edges matching. Stitch across lower edge, all along the back edge and along the opposite lower edge. Trim seam allowances, clip corners and turn right side out.

BRIGHT IDEA

Draped canopy Make a simple canopy by fitting curtain poles to the ceiling above the head and foot of the bed, and a third pole to the wall just above the bed. Measure from the head of the bed, up and over the poles, and add 2cm to allow for a 1m double section to hang at the foot with a casing for another pole.

5 Bind the leading edge
Use bias binding or bias-cut fabric strips to bind the front edge of the canopy (see page 82 for further information on bias-cut fabric strips). Turn under the ends of the binding to form a neat finish at each corner of the drape.

6 Make the casing △
Measure the circumference of the pole and divide by two. Fold the canopy in half across its width, right sides facing. Mark across the canopy to indicate half the circumference of the pole; tack the layers of the canopy together 5mm below this mark to allow a little ease so you can slip the canopy in place. Stitch along the tacked line and slip the canopy on to the pole.

◁ Empire line
A simple canopy, lined and bound in toning fabrics, creates a warm and welcoming effect over a single bed.

QUILTED BEDHEAD COVERS

Give a plain wooden, upholstered, or vinyl headboard a rich new look with a quilted slipover cover.

A headboard is a practical addition to any bed – as you will know if you have slept for any length of time in a bed *without* a headboard: the pillows fall behind the top of the bed, and the wall at the head of the bed gets marked.

A simple cover, made of quilted fabric, can be made to fit over almost any style of headboard. It can be made to co-ordinate with other furnishings, and has the advantage that it can be removed for washing.

The simplest and cheapest headboards are made of plywood or laminated chipboard – or you may have a padded one with a vinyl or fabric cover which is in need of renovation.

You will usually find that there are two struts down the back of the headboard, which are fixed to the base of the bed. Covering (or re-covering) a headboard made in this way is relatively straightforward – you can completely detach the headboard to make measuring and fitting easier.

CHOOSE YOUR FABRICS

A headboard cover, particularly if it is to go over a wooden bedhead, needs a certain amount of padding. The simplest answer is to use quilted fabric. If you cannot find a ready-quilted fabric to suit your decor, it is always possible to quilt ordinary fabric.

Choose a fabric to match or co-ordinate with existing furnishings: a complete co-ordinating set of bedlinen, bedspread and bedhead looks particularly effective. (Many companies now produce bedlinen to co-ordinate with their ranges of furnishing fabrics, which makes it much easier to achieve the desired effect.)

Quilting your own fabric If you are quilting your own fabric, choose a firmly-woven top fabric, medium-weight wadding, and a fairly lightweight, cheap fabric for the backing (as it will not show). Muslin or calico are suitable for this – the backing fabric is necessary to protect the wadding, both while you

are sewing and once the item has been made up.

Binding Because quilted fabric can be tricky to join neatly, it is best to bind the edges of the headboard together. Ready-made bias binding is too fine and too narrow for use in this case, so you will have to cut your own from matching, toning or contrasting un-quilted fabric 6cm wide.

MEASURING UP

To calculate the amount of fabric you need, measure the overall length and depth of the headboard. Add 6cm in each direction for a 1.5cm seam allowance and an extra allowance to enable you to ease the cover over the headboard and support battens.

If you are quilting your own fabric, you will need to allow a further 10cm all round, as quilting puffs up the fabric, so that it is slightly smaller when finished. Once the fabric is quilted you can cut it out accurately.

If the headboard has a curved or shaped top, you may find it easier to cut out a paper pattern first: simply trace the shape on to wall lining paper, then add the 3cm allowance all round when cutting out the fabric.

All padded out

This quilted slipover headboard cover is made up in a trellis fabric, which was quilted following the lines in the pattern. For added interest, decorative fabric panels have been quilted and topstitched to the cover.

QUILTING FABRIC

If you quilt the fabric yourself, you will have a much wider choice of patterns and colours. It entails a certain amount of preparation, and accurate stitching. Use a firmly woven fabric for the top fabric, medium-weight wadding and a lightweight fabric (e.g. muslin) for backing the quilting.

1 Join widths of fabric
If the item you are making is wider than the fabric width, join widths before you start, using a flat seam. Trim seam allowances and press seam open. Repeat for the backing fabric.

2 Join widths of wadding ▷
Join widths of wadding if necessary by butting the edges of the wadding together and stitching with a herringbone stitch.

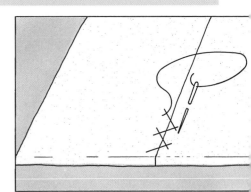

3 Cut out roughly
To save quilting a larger piece of fabric than you need, trim the top fabric, wadding and backing roughly to size – allowing 10cm all round, in addition to any seam allowances. This is because quilting puffs up the fabric slightly so that it seems to shrink.

4 Pin the layers together ◁
Lay out the backing fabric with the wadding on top of it and the top fabric on top of that, right side upwards. Pin together all round edges.

5 Tack the layers together ▷
Make lines of tacking stitches every 15cm in two directions across the fabric. (The tacking should run up and down for diagonal quilting, and diagonally if the quilting is to run up and down the fabric. This is to prevent the tacking getting caught too firmly in the quilting stitching.)

6 Mark the stitching lines
Use a ruler and dressmaker's chalk to mark the stitching lines over the whole panel to be quilted. These lines must be straight and accurately spaced.

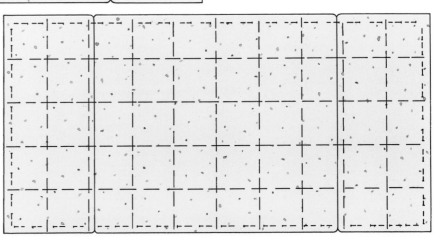

7 Machine stitch ◁
Stand your sewing machine on a fairly large table. This helps to stop the weight of the fabric pulling at the section that is being stitched, which could easily cause distortion. Feed the fabric through the sewing machine, rolling up the bulk so that you can handle it easily as you work. Make all the stitching lines in one direction first, and then the lines in the opposite direction.

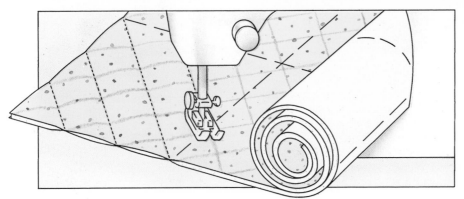

SLIPOVER HEADBOARD COVER

Whether you choose ready-quilted fabric or quilt the fabric yourself, the actual making-up of the headboard cover is the same. Instructions for quilting your own fabric are given opposite, and hints on using ready-quilted fabric are supplied overleaf.

1 *Draw up the pattern* ▷
Measure the headboard to be covered and, if it is a curved or intricate shape, draw up a pattern on pieces of lining paper, joined together if necessary. If you can remove the headboard, lay it on top of the paper on the floor and draw round it. If it is fixed, sketch out the shape on the paper, then hold it up against the headboard and adjust the shape to fit.

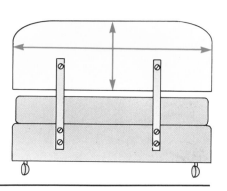

2 *Join widths of fabric*
If you are quilting your own fabric, cut out panels of fabric allowing an extra 13cm all round. Join widths if necessary, making vertical seams down the panels. (Use a full width of fabric in the centre and a narrower panel at each edge.) Quilt the fabric. Join widths of ready-quilted fabric if necessary before cutting out.

3 *Cut out the fabric*
Mark the dimensions of a straight headboard directly on to the quilted fabric with dressmaker's chalk, or pin the pattern in place. Cut out two identical panels, allowing 3cm all round for seams, and to ease the cover over the headboard. (If the headboard is more than a couple of centimetres thick, allow extra for ease.)

4 *Neaten the lower edge* ▽
Unpick the quilting stitches for 1.5cm along lower edge of each panel. Trim away 1.5cm of wadding and backing fabric along lower edges. Turn under 5mm along lower edge of top fabric, then turn up a further 1cm, over the raw edges of both wadding and backing fabric. Pin, tack and stitch in place close to inner edge.

5 *Prepare binding*
From plain fabric, cut out enough 6cm wide bias strips to go round sides and top of headboard panels. Remember to allow 1.5cm for seams if you have to join bias strips, and a couple of centimetres at each end. Join strips as necessary (see page 82 for more details on cutting and joining bias strips).

6 *Join the panels*
Lay out the front and back panels with wrong sides facing and raw edges matching. Pin, tack and stitch together round unfinished sides and top edge.

7 *Neaten the edges* ▷
Press under 1cm down each long edge of binding. Position binding round the side and top edge of the front of the bedhead, with right sides facing, so that the foldline of the binding matches the stitching line of the cover. Mitre the corners neatly. Pin, tack and stitch in place.

8 *Finish the binding*
Turn the binding over the raw edges of the fabric and pin in place just inside the stitching lines. Slipstitch in place, tucking in ends to neaten.

9 *Add ties* ▷
To hold the headboard cover in place, it is a good idea to add two pairs of ties to the lower edge. For each tie, cut a strip of fabric 6cm wide by 15cm long. Fold each tie in half down its length, with right sides facing. Pin, tack and stitch across one end and down one side, taking 1cm seams. Press. Trim seam allowances and clip corners. Turn

right side out and press. Turn in the raw edges and stitch across ends. Pin the neatened ends of the ties to each lower edge of headboard, spacing them evenly about a third of the way along it. Stitch the ties firmly in place. (Ensure that the ties do not coincide with the fixing battens at the back of the headboard.)

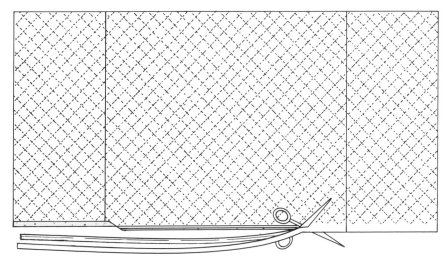

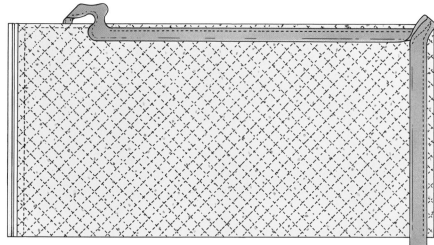

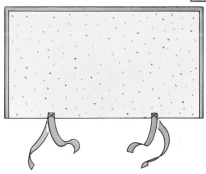

USING QUILTED FABRIC

If you choose to use ready-quilted fabric, here are some hints to help you get a good finish.

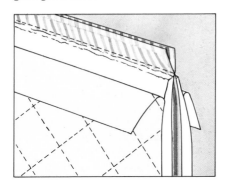

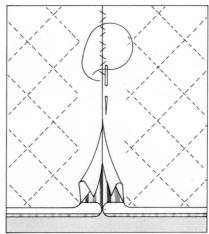

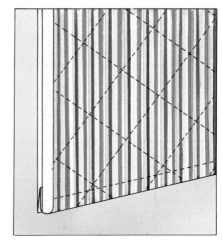

1 *Making a reversible seam △*
When working with reversible ready-quilted fabric (ie quilted fabric with top fabric on both sides, rather than a muslin backing), make a reversible seam. Unpick the quilting stitches for 3cm down each edge of the fabric panels to be joined. Do not trim the threads. Trim away 1.5cm of wadding down each edge. Make a flat seam through top fabric only.

2 *Finishing by hand △*
Press the seam open so that the seam allowance is folded over the wadding. Press under 1.5cm down lining fabric on both sides of seam. Butt the edges of the wadding together and herringbone stitch in place. Slipstitch the folded edges of the lining fabric together. For a neat finish, re-stitch the quilting by hand, using the loose ends and taking small backstitches.

Hemming △
Trimming the wadding from the hem reduces bulk. Unpick the quilting stitching from the hem allowance. Trim the wadding and lining fabric from the turn-up, then turn the hem over the lining, slipstitching it in place.

If you do not want the top fabric to show on the reverse side, allow just 1.5cm for the hem. Unpick 3cm of quilting all along the edge to be hemmed and trim away 1.5cm of wadding along that edge. Press under 1.5cm along the edge of the top fabric and the lining fabric, so that the seam allowance turns inside the quilted fabric. Slipstitch the folded edges together, or topstitch 5mm from folded edges.

Making a flat seam
If the fabric has a definite wrong side, make a flat seam. Unpick the quilting stitches in the seam allowance (usually 1.5cm). Trim away wadding from seam allowance. Pull ends of quilting stitching through to wrong side of fabric and knot them or position them so they will be stitched into the seam. Make a flat seam in the usual way, stitching through both the top fabric and the backing fabric. Press seam open.

▽ Headed with charm
A quilted slipover headboard cover and matching bedspread in washable fabric make a charming focal point in a child's bedroom.

BRIGHT IDEA

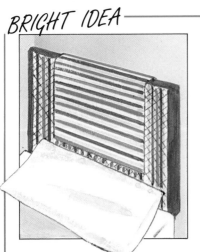

Keep it clean If you regularly sit up in bed, leaning against the headboard, it will get worn. Make a simple protector, which will be quick and easy to wash. Cut a piece of fabric to match the headboard, about 80cm square. Turn under a 1cm double hem all round the panel. Attach the hooked half of a piece of Velcro to the top of the panel, on the wrong side of the fabric, across its width, close to the edge. Attach the other half of the Velcro to the back of the headboard cover, near the top. Attach the fabric so it hangs over the headboard. Lean against it when you are reading (or watching TV), then flip it over the back when you have finished.

QUILTS AND FITTED BEDSPREADS

A good bedspread adds a smart and practical decorative touch to a bedroom, particularly if it is quilted.

In its simplest form, a bedspread is a piece of fabric which you throw over the bed to make it look tidy. Indeed, a simple cotton bedspread is one of the most economical choices. However, there are many more sophisticated styles, and these look particularly good if they are made up in fabrics to co-ordinate with other soft furnishings. If bedspreads are made up in crush-proof fabrics, there is the additional advantage that they can provide an extra layer on chilly nights – and they are very effective if they are quilted.

CHOOSE YOUR FABRICS

A firmly woven furnishing cotton is the best choice for a bedspread. Prints which match or tone with other fabrics in the room can look stunning. If you prefer a plain fabric, one with a textured weave will help to disguise creases and marks. It is a good idea to line any bedspread, to give it extra weight and help it to lie smoothly on the bed. Ordinary curtain lining fabric, which is available in a fair range of colours, is a good choice, or you could use sheeting fabric, to co-ordinate with existing bedlinen. Sheeting fabric also has the advantage that it is available in extra wide widths, reducing the amount of seaming involved. Bear in mind that the lining will show when the bedspread is turned back, so a colour to tone with trimmings is a good idea.

Trimmings Some styles of throwover bedspread can be made simply by joining widths of fabric and neatening the edge with cotton fringing. If you plan to use a cotton fringe, it is worth washing it before use, unless it is pre-shrunk.

Another trimming, particularly useful on quilted fabrics, is binding. You can either use ready-made binding, or for a more substantial finish, cut it on the cross from the same fabric as the bedspread. You could also use plain fabric for binding, in a colour to tone with a patterned fabric.

Piping is another useful trimming: again, if you are going to wash the bedspread regularly, it is advisable to pre-shrink the cord. Fairly chunky piping cord is best, because this will show up well against the large area of fabric in a bedspread. The position of the piping depends on the style of the bedspread. On a fitted bedspread, it is normal to insert piping round the edges of the main panel, to divide it from the skirt of the bedspread, so defining the shape of the bed. With a more casual throwover style, piping can be inserted all round the edge of the bedspread, between the fabric and the lining. In this case it is best to use a thick cord to form the piping. Alternatively, it can be used as an extra trimming to form a border set in from the edge of the quilt.

Soft options

Create a luxurious effect by making a thick, extravagantly proportioned throwover bedspread. For an extra decorative touch, the bedspread has been made up from several panels of fabric and the seams have been picked out in plain peach-coloured piping.

LINED THROWOVER BEDSPREAD

This simple throwover style is made up with contrasting piping stitched round the outer edge of the bedspread. The lining is locked in to the main fabric with long loose stitches, in the same way that lining is locked in to hand-made curtains.

CHECK YOUR NEEDS
- ☐ Main fabric
- ☐ Lining fabric (optional)
- ☐ Wadding (optional)
- ☐ Piping cord and fabric to cover
- ☐ Sewing thread
- ☐ Needles, pins
- ☐ Dressmaker's chalk
- ☐ Sewing machine (and piping foot)
- ☐ Sewing and cutting out scissors
- ☐ Tape measure
- ☐ Pencil and paper

1 Measure up ▷
Measure the bed with the usual bedclothes in place: measure the finished width required, from floor level on one side over the top of the bed and down to the floor on the other side. For the length, measure from the floor at the foot of the bed up to the bedhead, allowing plenty of 'ease' over the pillows. Add 3cm to each measurement for a 1.5cm seam allowance all round.

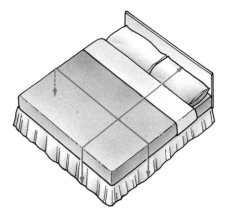

2 Calculate fabric amounts
The bedspread is made up from two widths of fabric: one central, full width panel with half a width joined to each side. The total length of fabric required is twice the length arrived at in Step 1, plus the same amount of lining fabric. With a patterned fabric, add an extra allowance for pattern matching. For piping, you will need enough chunky piping cord and bias strips to go down each side and across the foot of the bedspread.

3 Join fabric widths
Cut a length of fabric for the centre of the bedspread, the same as the length measurement in Step 1. Cut the remaining piece of fabric in half down its length, then pin and tack to either side of the first piece: selvedges should match, and right sides should be facing. Stitch and press seams open. Repeat to join widths of lining.

4 Trim to size
Measure the width of the made-up panel of main fabric and trim to the width arrived at in Step 1. Trim the lining to match.

5 Prepare the piping ▷
Measure round the piping cord and add 3cm. Cut bias strips to this width. Join sufficient lengths of piping to make up a strip long enough to cover the cord. Bias strips can be difficult to join.

See page 82 for details of the method used to solve this problem and for information on cutting continuous bias strips. Wrap the bias strip over the cord and pin, tack and stitch in place, using a piping foot.

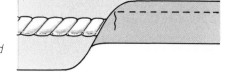

6 Round off the base corners ◁
Use a large dinner plate to round off the two base corners of the main panel of the bedspread. Mark the curves with dressmaker's chalk and then trim away the fabric outside the marked line. Trim the lining to match.

7 Position and stitch the piping ▷
Position the piping round the sides and lower edge of the right side of the fabric so that the raw edges match. Tack in place, then stitch close to the cord, starting to stitch 2cm from the top edge of the fabric. Clip into the seam allowance of the piping at the corners so that it lies flat. Press, and then turn the raw edges to the inside and press again so that the piping sits neatly at the edge of the fabric. Trim the cord at the ends so that it is 1.5cm shorter than its casing. Turn in the raw edges at the ends of the bias strips and slipstitch together. Note that the neatened ends of the piping fall short of the raw edge of the top of the bedspread by 1.5cm (the seam allowance).

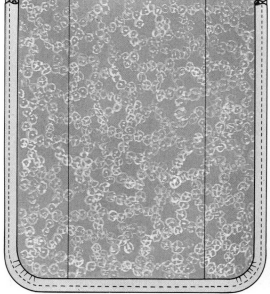

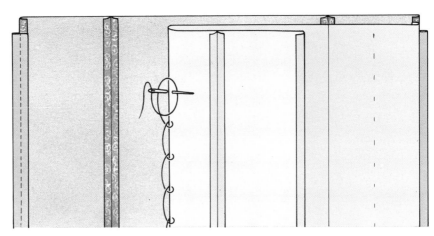

8 Lock in the lining ▷
Turn under and press 1.5cm down the sides and across the lower edge of the lining. Position the lining on top of the bedspread with wrong sides facing, so that all the raw edges are sandwiched between the panels of fabric. Pin in place down seam lines on main panel and in the centre of the bedspread. Lay out on a flat surface, with lining facing you, then turn back the lining down the left-hand side. Lock the lining to the main fabric down the seam lines every 40cm across the width.

9 Finish the edges ◁
Finally, slipstitch the folded edge of the lining to the piping cord, close to the existing lines of stitching. Cut notches in the curved seam allowance so that it sits neatly. Turn in and press 1.5cm across the top edge of both the main fabric and the lining. Slipstitch folded edges together. Press.

Note: If you do not wish to have piping round the edge, add an 8cm allowance to the width and a 5.5cm allowance to the length of the bedspread in Step 1 (4cm down the sides and across the lower edge, 1.5cm across the top edge.) Join the panels of fabric as before, then turn under and press 4cm down sides and lower edge. Herringbone stitch raw edges in place. Turn under 2cm down the sides and lower edge of the lining. Position lining on fabric, wrong sides facing, so that raw edges match across the top, and the folded edge of the lining is 5mm inside the folded edge of the main fabric. Pin fabric together and lock in the lining as before. Slipstitch the edge of the lining in place then turn in 1.5cm across the top edge of both the lining and the main piece of fabric and slipstitch as before.

IDEAS FOR QUILTED COVERS

A simple quilted cover Make up the top and lining as for the lined throwover. Cut and butt-join polyester wadding to make up a panel which is 2cm smaller all round than the main panel. Tack the wadding to the wrong side of the main panel, positioning it centrally. Lay the lining fabric on the right side of the main panel, ensuring the raw edges are matching all round. Quilt the fabric through both layers (see pages 63-64). Trim the raw edges if necessary and round off corners at the lower edge. Then bind with bias-cut strips.

Outline quilting For an extra personal touch, you can quilt the fabric following the lines of the pattern, so long as it is not too intricate. (A simple stripe looks very effective if you position the quilting along the lines of the stripe.)

Geometric panels For extra elegance, make up the top panel with diagonal seams. Plan the arrangement on graph paper first to avoid wasting fabric (right). Piping along the seams adds an interesting touch.

Make up the panel so that it is 10cm larger all round than the finished measurement. Turn under and press 1cm and then a further 9cm all round top panel. Cut lining fabric to the

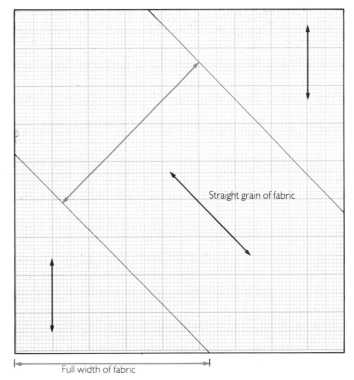

Straight grain of fabric

Full width of fabric

finished size, joining widths as necessary. Cut wadding to the same size as the lining, butt-joining widths if necessary. Sandwich the wadding between the lining and the top fabric, with right sides facing outwards. Tack together all round edges. Turn hem allowance of top fabric over edge of wadding and lining and pin and tack in place, mitring corners neatly. Topstitch 8.5cm from edge of quilt down sides and across lower edge to form a neat border.

FITTED BEDSPREAD

This bedspread has a lined top panel, piping round the edge of the top panel, and a straight skirt with box pleats at the corners. The instructions are for a single bed: for a double bed, follow the same technique, adding extra seams in the top panel. Measure the overall size and height of the bed over the normal bedclothes.

1 *The overall measurements* ▷
For the top panel, add a 1.5cm seam allowance to the overall size. For the depth of the skirt, add 1.5cm for seams and 5cm for the hem. For the length of the side skirt, add 3cm for seams/hems and 10cm for the pleat; for the end skirt add 3cm for seams and 20cm for pleats. For pleat panels you will need two pieces the depth of the skirt by 23cm.

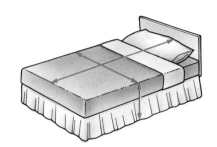

2 *Calculate fabric amounts*
Draw up a cutting plan so that you can calculate the total amount of fabric needed. Normally the fabric is cut so that the straight grain runs down the length of the bed and vertically down the skirt panels. You will find that you have to join widths of fabric to make up the side skirt panels of the bedspread, unless you choose to have the grain

running along the length of the skirt. Include an allowance for bias strips to make up matching piping (or buy contrasting fabric for this), and allow for pattern matching where necessary. You will need enough piping to go along the sides and across the base of the top panel. For lining, you will need a panel of fabric the same size as the top panel in Step 1.

3 *Make up the skirt*
Cut out side and end panels for the skirt, making seams as necessary. Cut out pleat lining panels. Turn up a 2.5cm wide double hem along the lower edge of each section. Join the skirt sections with french seams. Join them in the following order: side, pleat panel, end, pleat, side. Do not press seams open.

4 *Neaten the ends of the skirt*
Turn under 5mm and then a further 1cm at each end of the skirt; pin, tack and stitch in place.

5 *Make the pleats* ▷
Fold back and press a 10cm turning at each end of the end skirt panel and at pleat ends of side panels. This forms the box pleat. Tack the pleat in place across the top.

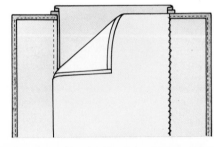

6 *Prepare the piping*
Cut bias strips to suit the piping cord, allowing a total of 3cm seam allowance. Cover the piping cord as usual. Position the piping round the sides and lower edge of the right side of the top panel, and pin, tack and stitch in place. Press raw edges to inside. Trim piping cord 1.5cm from top edge of panel. Clip into the seam allowance of the piping at the corners.

7 *Attach the skirt*
Position the skirt round the piped edge of the top panel of the bedspread so that raw edges match and piping is sandwiched between them. Make sure that the centre of the pleats match the corners of the top panel. Pin, tack and stitch in place.

8 *Fit the lining panel* ◁
Turn under 1.5cm all round lining panel. Place lining on top panel, wrong sides facing with fold line 1.5cm from top of top panel. Slipstitch folded edge of lining to seam allowance of piping, close to first stitching line. Turn under and press 1.5cm across top of bedspread and slipstitch to lining.

BRIGHT IDEA

SOFTER STYLE
For a fitted bedspread with a softer look, follow the instructions given for the fitted valance on pages 72-73, measuring over the bedclothes rather than under the mattress. You can add piping and a lining as for the fitted bedspread.

◁ *Keep it smart*
A tailored bedspread gives a classic finish to a bed. The seersucker fabric is a practical choice, as it resists creasing and can therefore be used as an extra layer in cold weather. Large pillows and a bolster have been covered to match the bedspread.

MAKING YOUR OWN BEDLINEN

Bedlinen is very easy to make and you can adapt the techniques to suit different styles and sizes of bed.

Although there seems to be an ever-increasing range of ready-made bedlinen in the shops, there are many reasons for making your own. The first is economy: although the cost of making your own bedlinen may be equal to the cost of lower quality ready-mades, the sheeting available by the metre is of much better quality than that used for cheap ready-made bedlinen, so that you can be sure it will stay crisper longer.

You may also have unusual sized beds (whether they are narrow bunks or king-sized beds) so that your choice of ready-made bedlinen is limited or non-existent. And thirdly, you can customize your bedlinen to match your decor exactly, adding contrasting frills or appliqued patterns, or even using fabrics which were not intended for bedlinen, but match other furnishings.

CHOOSE YOUR FABRIC

Sheeting is available by the metre in major department stores and some specialist furnishing shops. It is normally made of cotton or a cotton/polyester mix, either plain or patterned. You can even buy fabric to make your own silk sheets. Standard widths for sheeting are 175cm, 228/230cm and 275cm. It is advisable to use these wider fabrics for sheets and the underside of duvet covers so that there are no uncomfortable seams. But there is no reason why you can't use other fabrics for pillow-slips and the tops of duvet covers, as long as they are closely woven, hard-wearing and washable. It is worth pre-shrinking fabrics which are not sold as sheeting to prevent shrinkage and distortion after the item has been sewn.

Extras You will also need sewing thread (cotton for cotton fabrics and synthetic for polyester) and fasteners to close the opening of the duvet cover. Choose from press-fastening tape (plastic or metal press-studs already attached to lightweight tapes), individual press-fasteners, strips or spots of Velcro, buttons, tie tapes or even long zips. In the example here, we give instructions for using a tape with plastic press-studs.

Summer freshness
Crisp cool colours bring a breath of fresh air in the bedroom. Sheeting material is available in a wide range of colours: here several patterns in the same colour mix and match successfully.

BED	SIZE	FLAT SHEET	DUVET COVER
Cot	60 × 120cm	116 × 176cm	100 × 120cm
Single bed	75/90 × 190cm	180 × 260cm	135 × 200cm
Double bed	135 × 190cm	230 × 260cm	200 × 200cm
King-size bed	No standard	275 × 275cm	220 × 230cm

MEASURING UP

Check the size of your bed before you start. If you are making fitted sheets, also measure the depth of the mattress, and for valances measure the height of the bed base. The chart indicates the standard sizes you may come across.

MAKING A FLAT SHEET

Always measure up carefully before buying sheeting fabric. Measure the top of the mattress in both directions, and add the depth of the mattress all round, plus a generous allowance for tuck-ins and hems.

1 *Cut out the fabric*
Cut one piece of sheeting to the required size: follow the chart above for standard bed sizes, adding an allowance of 20cm to the length for hems. If the selvedges are not used as side hems, add 4cm to the finished width measurement to allow for seams.

2 *Finish the side edges*
Where possible, use the selvedges as the side edges of the sheet. However, if the sheeting is more than 10cm wider than the finished size, you will have to cut and hem the edges. Turn under 1cm, then a further 1cm to make a double hem. Pin, tack and stitch in place down each side.

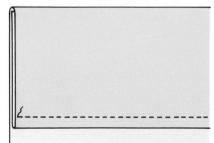

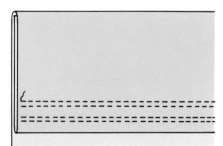

3 *Finish the lower edge △*
At the foot of the sheet, turn under 2cm and then a further 2cm to form a 2cm double hem. Pin, tack and stitch close to the edge of the hem.

4 *Hem the top edge △*
Turn under 8cm and then a further 8cm to make a double hem. Pin, tack and stitch, positioning the stitching 7mm from the inner edge of the hem. (Take particular care, as this is the only part of the hem which will show when the sheet is in use as a top sheet.)

5 *Making a corded edge △*
For a decorative finish, you can add cording: make a second row of stitching 3mm from the first (1cm from the inner edge of the hem) to make a channel for the cord. Make two further rows of stitching, 3mm apart, starting 7mm from the first channel, as shown. With a tapestry needle, thread cord through each channel. Hand-stitch ends in place.

MAKING A FRILLED VALANCE

When in use, most of the flat section of the valance does not show as it is under the mattress. You could economize by making the central part of the flat section of the valance from a remnant of fabric or an old sheet.

1 *Measure up and cut out*
Measure the length, width and height of the bed base. For the top of the valance, add 3.5cm to the length and 3cm to the width, and cut out a piece of fabric to these measurements. For the depth of the frill, add 6.5cm to the

height of the base; for the length of the frill, add together twice the length of the bed, plus the width and multiply by two. Cut out enough widths of fabric to make up a frill to this measurement: since it will be gathered, you need not be absolutely precise.

2 *Curve the lower corners ▷*
Curve the two base corners of the flat part of the valance by positioning a plate at one corner and drawing round it with dressmaker's chalk. Fold the fabric in half lengthwise, pin corners together, and cut out through both layers of fabric following guide line.

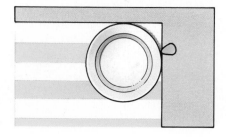

3 *Make up the frill*
Pin and stitch the short edges of the frill pieces together using french seams, taking first a 5mm and then a 1cm seam allowance. To hem the frill, turn under 2.5cm all along one long edge, and then a further 2.5cm to form a double hem. Pin, tack and stitch.

4 Gather up the frill ▷
This is easier if you work in sections. Along the top edge of the frill, make five evenly spaced marks to give six equal sections. Work two rows of gathering stitch in each section. Divide up the three sides of the flat panel to which the frill will be sewn into six equal sections and mark.

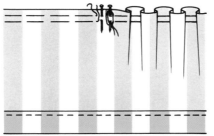

5 Add the frill
Pin the frill round the sides and base of the flat panel, with right sides together, matching the marks. Pull up each set of gathering stitches in turn to fit the corresponding part of the top and tack in place. Stitch all round, taking 1.5cm seams. Trim the seam allowance to 1cm and zigzag stitch the raw edges together to neaten them.

6 Hem the top edge ◁
Turn under a double 1cm hem along the top edge of the flat panel and along the frill on each side. Pin, tack and stitch in place.

MAKING A FITTED SHEET

Fitted sheets have the advantage of staying taut on the bed, so that bed-making is easier and the sheet does not ruck up at night. Measure your mattress before you start: the depth will affect the amount of fabric you need and the way you stitch the corners.

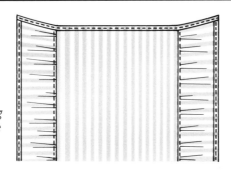

1 Cut out the fabric
The length of fabric needed is equal to the length of the mattress plus twice the depth plus 18cm at each end for tuck in and hems. The width needed is the width of the mattress plus twice the depth plus 18cm at each side for tuck in and hems. Cut out one piece of fabric to these measurements.

2 Mark the corner darts △
Calculate the position of the corner darts by adding 18cm (tuck in and hem allowance) to the depth of the mattress. Measure and mark this amount along each edge on either side of each corner. Mark a line at right angles to the edge at each marked point and mark where the lines meet.

3 Cut and stitch the darts △
Cut out the corner of the sheet 1.5cm inside the marked lines. With wrong sides facing and marked lines matching, pin, tack and stitch to make a french seam, taking a 5mm and then a 1cm seam allowance.

4 Hem the outer edge
Turn under 1.5cm all round the outer edge of the sheet, and then a further 1.5cm. Pin and tack in place. Mark the hem 35cm from each corner dart on each side. Stitch hem, leaving a 1.5cm opening at each marked point.

5 Gather up the corners
Cut four 25cm lengths of narrow elastic. Pin one end of one piece of elastic to the hem at an opening. Using a safety pin, thread the opposite end of the elastic through the hem round the corner and out at the next opening. Pin

to hold both ends in place. Repeat for all the other openings and then make two rows of stitching across the hem at each end of each length of elastic to hold it firmly in position, and complete the hem stitching.

MAKING A PILLOWCASE

1 Cut out the fabric
For a standard (74cm × 48cm) pillow, cut a strip of fabric across the width of the sheeting 178cm × 53cm.

2 Hem the short edges
On one short edge (which will be tucked in) turn under 5mm and then a further 5mm for a double hem. Pin, tack and stitch in place. On the other short

edge, turn under 6cm and then a further 6cm and pin, tack and stitch in place. For a decorative finish, make a double row of cording as described for flat sheets.

3 Form the flap ▷
Lay out the fabric, wrong side up. At the end with a narrow hem, turn under 15cm to form a flap. Pin and tack in place along raw edges.

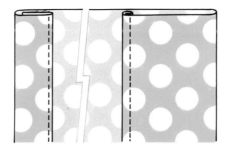

4 Complete the pillowcase
Fold the pillowcase in half, wrong sides together, so that the wide hemmed edge matches the fold of the flap. To make french seams, pin and stitch both long edges, taking 5mm seams. Turn pillowcase inside out and press. Pin and stitch the second part of the french seam, taking 1cm seams.

MAKING A DUVET COVER

A plain duvet cover is easily made from a few metres of fabric. Sheeting is available in suitably wide widths, but other fabrics can be used for the top, where seams won't disturb sleepers.

1 *Cut out the fabric*
Measure the duvet and add 9cm to the length and 3cm to the width to allow for seams. Cut out two pieces of fabric to these dimensions.

2 *Make the hems*
At the base edge of each piece, turn under 1.5cm and then a further 1.5cm to make a double hem. Pin and stitch in place.

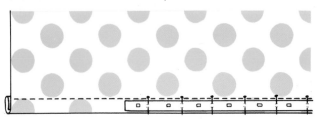

3 *Fit the fastenings △*
Measure and mark 15cm in from side edges along each neatened lower edge. Pin and tack strips of press-fasteners to the right side of each neatened edge, between marks, ensuring fasteners match. Stitch in place.

4 *Stitch the bottom seam △*
Fasten both parts of the duvet cover together with the press-fasteners: the right sides of the fabric should be facing, with raw edges matching all round. The bottom seam is a simple flat seam (the seam allowances are already

neatened). Pin and tack seams at each end of opening, positioning the stitching just inside fold line of hem. Make the seam line 16cm long, and continue it across the seam allowance, so that the ends of the fastening are held firmly. Stitch seams.

5 *Stitch the sides and top*
Turn duvet cover so that it is right side out. Pin, tack and stitch side and top seams, taking 5mm seam allowance. Press. Clip seam allowance at corners. Turn inside out, press, and finish french seam, taking 1cm seam allowance.

▽ Cheerful for children
Making bedlinen can be a real economy in a child's bedroom. Here a bold pattern has been used for the duvet and pillowcase, and a smaller pattern for the sheet and valance.

BRIGHT IDEA

TAILORED FINISH
For a less frilly valance, you can use straight panels of fabric for the skirt: cut sufficient strips to make up a valance to fit round the sides and foot of the flat panel, adding an extra 80cm to make two inverted pleats. Mark the position of the pleats to fit at the corners and tack them in place before stitching the straight skirt to the flat section. Finish the top edge as for the frilled version.

UPHOLSTERY FABRICS

There's a wide choice of fabrics — varying in quality and texture — for both close and loose chair covers.

The first decision that needs to be made when buying new seating or re-covering old, is whether to have tight or loose covers. Sometimes it is the piece of furniture that dictates the choice, sometimes it is the fabric itself. In some instances tight upholstery is the only option: on dining chairs, for example, or fully upholstered seating with curved outlines and buttoned detailing. And if the types of fabric you like are velvets, tweeds, or some of the new tapestries and epinglé weaves then again, tight upholstery is the only choice as these fabrics are too bulky for loose covers.

Tailored loose covers give a neat, streamlined fit to sofas and chairs and they have the advantage of being easy to remove if a serious spillage threatens to stain them. Once again, there are limitations on the type of fabric that is suitable. Only materials which are reasonably light and pliable can be successfully made into loose covers. The traditional choice is linen union in which hardwearing flax is woven together with cotton. Nowadays, many manufacturers add approximately 10% of synthetic yarn, such as nylon, to strengthen the softer cotton and make it more suitable for use with flax fibre which is quite abrasive and can wear through the cotton if it is subjected to heavy wear.

Fabrics which wear best in loose covers are closely woven weaves in which there is an exact balance between warp and weft. A strong, closely-woven cotton print will, in many cases, wear better in loose covers than a linen union, despite the fact that it may feel thinner and less sturdy.

Manufacturers of furniture designed to take loose covers always recommend that the covers should be dry cleaned rather than washed. Fabrics cannot always be pre-shrunk reliably and, if the piping shrinks at a different rate from the fabric, it will pucker along the main seam lines. The maximum shrinkage allowed under British Standards is a total of 6% and if even this small amount were to spoil the look of your furniture, you would have no grounds for complaint.

Retaining its good looks is such an important factor with upholstery that many fabrics are now being offered with a soil-resistant finish which prevents particles of dirt and fluids from penetrating the fibres. Spills are kept floating on the surface, temporarily at least, giving you the chance to mop them up rather than see them sink disastrously — and in many cases permanently — into the weave.

There are many weights and styles of cloth that can be used for covers but they do not all offer the same potential for hard wear. A sofa in a family living room takes heavy punishment compared with an easy chair in a bedroom. The need for quality is also affected by fashion in textiles and interiors. So if you are fashion conscious, think carefully before spending large sums of money on highly expensive, very durable fabric. However, if you are not particularly fashion minded, paying for good quality cloth is a worthwhile step.

FABRICS, WEAVES AND FINISHES

When you are selecting a particular fabric for your upholstery, you must consider not only the colour and pattern of the fabric, but also the weave, the fibre or yarn the fabric is made from and the weight of the cloth.

△ COTTON CHINTZ
Attractive when used for loose covers or upholstery but it should be regarded as a light-duty cloth suitable for bedroom chairs or for use in an adult drawing room. The word 'chintz' is Hindu and used to describe fairly bright patterns; it now often refers to fabrics with a shiny or glazed finish.

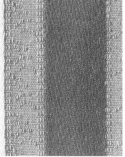

△ BROCADE
This is similar to damask (see overleaf) except that it is always woven in more than two colours, so that the pattern is more clearly defined. It is usually a blend of viscose with cotton and sometimes silk and linen.

▷ COTTON PRINT AND PLAIN WEAVE
Firmly woven cottons, either printed or plain, are good for light-duty upholstery and wear well when made up as loose covers. Some much heavier duty printed cottons are now available: they look similar to linen union (see overleaf) but lack the distinctive slub.

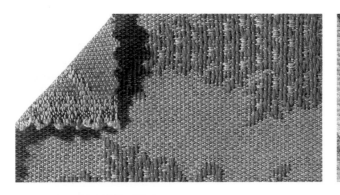

△ COTTON JACQUARD

This is a self-patterned fabric (in which the pattern is actually woven into the cloth). It is similar to a cotton weave but the woven element allows more colours to be used. The fact that the 'negative' of the pattern shows on the reverse of the fabric can sometimes be used decoratively.

△ COTTON TWILL

Generally a heavyweight cloth with a strong diagonal in the weave, running from selvedge to selvedge. Examine the fabric before use to make sure you know which is the 'right' side.

△ COTTON WEAVE

This is available in either pure cotton or a blend of cotton and another fibre such as viscose. Viscose is added to give lustre to the cloth, as well as strength. The pattern results from a combination of the shape of the weave and the colours which are used.

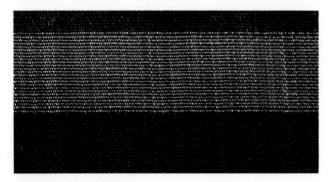

△ CREWELWORK

This is a form of embroidery traditionally worked in wool worsted on heavy, natural cotton cloth. The design is usually a tree of life, bursting with flowers and birds. This decorative cloth has been used for covers and bedhangings since the 15th century.

△ DAMASK

A weave most frequently found in pure cotton but traditionally made in silk or wool. A design is woven to appear matt and slightly raised against a satin ground. A single colour may be used, or two closely toning colours, giving a very subtle effect. Usually in traditional – often floral – designs, some unchanged since the 16th century, damask is suitable for loose covers and medium-duty upholstery. As with other woven patterns, make sure you use it 'right' side out as the satin ground is more hard wearing than the more knobbly reverse.

△ DOBBY WEAVE

This weave is characterized by a small, self-coloured raised motif (often a diamond shape, trellis or spot) and is usually woven in cotton or a cotton blend. It is a style which has been in use since the 18th century, and is suited to loose covers and light or medium-duty upholstery.

◁ HORSEHAIR

A highly traditional cloth used since the 18th and 19th centuries; both Chippendale and Hepplewhite mention it as a cloth favoured for covering their chairs. It is not suitable for

HORSEHAIR (continued)

loose covers or fully upholstered armchairs or sofas. The horsehair is used only for the weft (crosswise threads) with a continuous warp of cotton running lengthwise. Horsehair is made in traditional stripes and sateens as well as small damask prints.

△ LEATHER AND LEATHER-LOOK PVC

A very hardwearing – but fairly expensive – material for covering furniture. Some leathers are waterproof (or wipeable), while others are likely to carry watermarks, so check the finish when buying. Leather and PVC are both very hardwearing as upholstery fabrics but can be damaged by animal claws. Be wary of leather-look PVC fabrics which may feel uncomfortably hot if you sit on them for long periods.

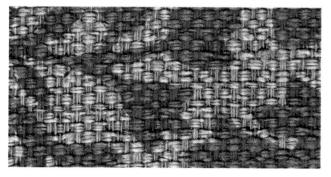

△ LINEN

Linen is the name given to yarn spun from natural flax, and to fabrics woven from linen thread. It is a fabric which has been in use in this country for centuries: finer weaves for clothing, table and bedlinen, and coarser weaves for furnishing fabrics. It is the most hardwearing natural fibre of all but has one major drawback – it creases badly. There are a few heavy, pure linen cloths available which are suitable for tight upholstery where creasing is not a problem since the fabric is pulled and fixed into place and does not move.

△ LINEN UNION

A blend of linen with cotton, which is available in both plain colours and patterns, either floral or geometric. The addition of the cotton makes a softer cloth that is less prone to creasing. Over the last few decades, a little synthetic yarn has often been added to improve its wear.

△ MATELASSÉ

This is a self-coloured fabric, woven to create pockets. The weaving technique makes it look slightly padded or quilted. It is often woven in a blend of fibres such as cotton and viscose (the synthetic fibre improves wear). It is a bulky fabric, and can be difficult to make into loose covers.

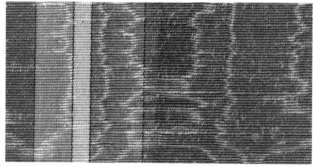

△ MOIRÉ

This term is used to describe a watermarked fabric mostly used for curtains. Originally, the markings were applied to mohair, but the technique became commonly used for silk. Nowadays there are heavy-duty moiré plains and stripes designed for upholstery; those with a high linen content are the most hard wearing. In many modern fabrics, the effect is printed or woven on the fabric.

TESTS FOR UPHOLSTERY FABRICS

Don't be tempted to save a few pounds and buy a fabric that isn't suitable for upholstery (even if you adore the design). There are stringent tests to which manufacturers subject their fabrics to ensure they are hardwearing and suitable for the job in hand. The guidelines for the following tests are laid down by British Standard BS 2543.

The Martindale Abrasion Test – also known as the rub test – is carried out on woven fabrics but not on knitted cloths. The test determines whether the fabric is suitable for upholstery by measuring how quickly it wears out under the rub test. A cloth that wears (when three threads are broken) after 6,000 rubs is considered only suitable for light domestic use while a fabric suitable for medium or heavy wear will have to withstand 15,000–20,000 rubs.

The Colourfast to Light Test determines how quickly the fabric's colours will fade when subjected to intense light. This test is particularly important if you want to have matching curtains and upholstery.

The Visible Soiling Test determines how easily a fabric soils and ensures that unpleasant marks are not left on your furniture when it comes in contact with clammy hands or sweaty bodies.

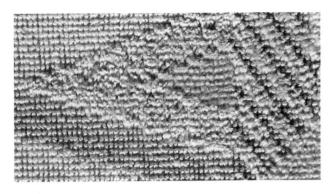

△ MOQUETTE

A loop pile cloth usually woven on a cotton base with cut and uncut pile in cotton, wool or linen. The cloth was often used for the 'Jazz' patterns of the 1930s.

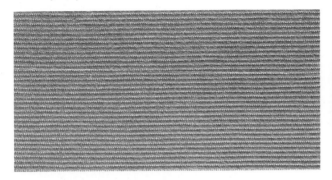

△ OTTOMAN

A tightly woven cloth with a horizontal corded rib. The name, which comes from Turkey, traditionally refers to a silk cloth used to cover a low stuffed seat. It is now generally woven in pure cotton or a cotton/viscose blend. It is reasonably hard wearing and suitable for both loose covers and tight upholstery.

△ TWEED

Traditionally woven in pure wool, this is a soft, hard wearing upholstery cloth. Modern tweeds are often blended with synthetic fibres for extended wear, or made entirely from man-made fibres.

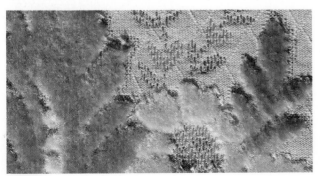

△ EPINGLÉ

This is the French version of moquette and is usually made of cotton with well-defined loops. Patterns are usually geometric or other fairly simple designs. Neither moquette nor epinglé is suitable for loose covers, and they are both to be avoided if you have cats!

△ TAPESTRY

This fabric is usually woven on a cotton base and can be pure cotton, or a mix of cotton and viscose or wool. There are many inexpensive tapestry cloths that are comparatively lightweight and would only give medium-duty wear. Heavy tapestries are one of the most hardwearing materials for upholstery. Colours are usually fairly dark and practical: the pattern is created by both the weave and the different coloured warp threads.

△ VELVET

Velvet has been used for upholstery and curtains for centuries. Traditionally it was woven in cotton, but the most widely used quality now is high lustre acrylic velvet best known by the trade name Dralon. Never use curtain grade velvets for covering chairs. Linen velvet is another – very expensive – type of velvet. The low lustre pile is longer than acrylic velvet.

◁ FIGURED VELVET

Figured velvet is woven on jacquard looms that combine tapestry and pile in one cloth. It is not suitable for loose covers, but is frequently used, in combination with plain velvet, for upholstery.

MAKING LOOSE COVERS

When sofas and chairs have soft, curved lines, you need a little more skill to make tight-fitting loose covers.

Loose covers are one type of home sewing which you should not tackle unless you have some experience in sewing. Many of the techniques employed are similar to those used in dressmaking, particularly when it comes to fitting covers to curved, softly shaped chairs and sofas, rather than to simple square shaped furniture. However, it is well worth tackling these more difficult shapes if you have done quite a lot of home sewing or dressmaking, and can find a suitable, reasonably priced fabric.

One of the great advantages of covering furniture with removable loose covers is that you can co-ordinate a motley assortment of second-hand chairs and sofas. You can create quite striking effects through the clever use of toning fabrics. You could, for example, use one colour for the main part of a cover with a contrasting colour for piping, and reverse the colours for another chair in the same room. You can also choose the trimmings, such as piping and skirts, to suit the style of the room in which the chairs stand.

FABRICS AND TRIMMINGS

Always choose tightly woven fabrics for loose covers. Avoid very bulky fabrics unless you have a heavy-duty sewing machine. The most usual fastenings are strips of Velcro, and you will also need tapes to tie the cover in place under the chair or sofa. If you plan to insert piping along the seams, you also need no. 5 piping cord as well as bias-cut strips of fabric (see the instructions on page 82 for details of cutting large quantities of bias binding).

PATTERN MAKING

If you are at all worried about making up loose covers, it is worth making a pattern first: use old sheeting, remnants of fabric, or old curtains (jumble sales are a good source). You can always keep the patterns to use as dust covers next time you are decorating! If you are replacing a loose cover which has worn beyond repair, you can make the job easier by taking this apart and using it as a pattern.

Making a pattern also makes it easier to position motifs on heavily patterned fabric when you cut it out. For example, if the fabric you use has a bold motif, it should be centrally positioned on cushions and back panels. If there is a border, you might want to arrange this round the skirt of the chair or sofa, or down the front panel of the arms.

Fresh new look
This pretty little sofa has been covered in an attractive floral fabric with contrasting piping in peach to match the scatter cushions. A crisply pleated frill adds an individual touch to the skirt.

MEASURING UP

As with simpler shapes, start by dividing the chair into sections and decide where all the seams are to go. Normally it is easiest to follow the seams on the existing cover. At the same time, decide which seams you intend to insert piping into.

1 Measure at maximum points
Measure each section of the chair or sofa at its maximum point. Add 10cm to each measurement for seam allowances. Add an extra 15cm to any edges which are tucked in round the seat and back of the chair. For a cover without a skirt, allow an extra 20cm along lower edges of back, sides and front of seat; this is to make a casing so you can thread tape through it and tie the cover under the chair or sofa. For a cover with a skirt, omit the seam allowance at lower edge. Decide depth of the skirt and calculate the fabric needed for the skirt, and for a panel to make a casing along each lower edge. Don't forget to measure any loose cushions.

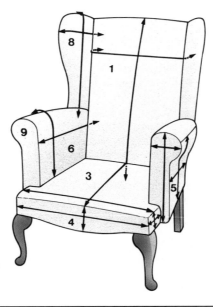

2 Cut out the pattern pieces
Use these measurements to cut out rectangles for the pattern pieces. Label them clearly. Calculate the exact quantities of fabric only after you have trimmed the pattern pieces to shape.

1 Inner back
2 Outer back (behind chair)
3 Seat
4 Front seat
5 Outer arm (cut two)
6 Inner arm (cut two)
7 Outer wing (cut two)
8 Inner wing (cut two)
9 Arm gussets (cut two)
Plus seat cushion panels

FITTING THE PATTERN

Make up the pattern to fit half the chair or sofa. Then pin out the pieces on folded fabric, or reverse the pattern pieces as necessary, to ensure that the two halves of the chair or sofa match.

1 Mark the centre line ◁
Mark a line down the centre of the chair or sofa using dressmaker's chalk: up the outside back, down the inside back, across seat and down front seat.

2 Position the inside back panel ▷
Fold the pattern piece for the inside back in half down its length. Position the fold line on the chalk mark, and arrange the panel so that the tuck-in allowances overlap the seat and the arm as appropriate. Pin it in place.

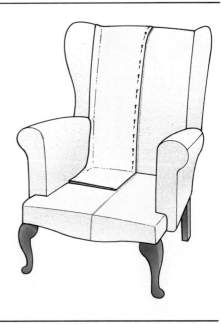

3 Adjust the shape to fit ▷
Round the top of the chair, trim the pattern to follow the curve of the back, leaving a 2cm seam allowance. Where the back is a full, rounded shape, you will need to take tucks or make small gathers in the cover to fit round the curves. Clip into seam allowance round the curve where back meets the arm.

4 Shape the remaining panels
Repeat to shape the back, inside and outside arms, seat and front seat sections, marking the seam lines as you go. Check the seams match, following the seam lines on the existing cover.

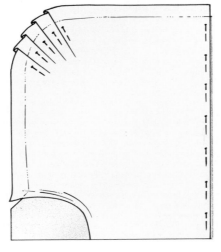

5 Fitting the wings
Every style of chair is made in a slightly different way, so it is difficult to generalize, but on most wing chairs there is a small tuck-in between the back of the chair and the inside of the wing. There may also be a small tuck-in between the lower edge of the inside of the wing and the top of the inside of the arm. When fitting, make an allowance for these tuck-ins according to their size. You will usually have to gather the fabric to fit round the curved top of the wings. Go on pinning and adjusting the pattern until you are satisfied with the fit.

6 Scroll arms ▷
There are many different shapes for the front of the arms of a chair. It may simply be a question of cutting the front panel to a simple curved shape (near right), or you may find that it is more effective to gather or pleat the fabric over the front of the arm, fitting a shaped front panel inside the gathered edge (far right).

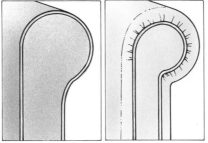

7 Check the fit
When all the pieces are pinned in place, with seam lines marked and pinned in place around the edges where appropriate, check that there is no distortion or puckering of any of the panels. Check, too, that the cover is not so tight round curved sections that you cannot slip it on and off the chair. Mark the position of the opening.

8 Remove the pattern pieces
Remove the pattern pieces from the chair or sofa, and start to unpin the seams. Mark each end of any gathered sections and make corresponding marks on the opposite seam line so that you can transfer the marks to the actual panels of fabric when you cut them out. Finally, unpin any remaining seams and flatten them out.

9 Plan a cutting layout
To calculate the actual amount of fabric for the cover, you can make a scale diagram showing the width of the fabric by two parallel lines. Ensure they lie along the straight grain of the fabric. You could also lay out the pattern pieces on the floor. Mark two lines on the floor to represent the width of the fabric you plan to use. Using pins or

dressmaker's chalk (which you can vacuum up later), draw any border and/or pattern repeat on the floor. Lay out the pattern pieces: ensure they are the right way up and position motifs and borders appropriately. Position the centre back, centre front and centre seat panels on folded fabric, so that the centre of the pattern piece is on the fold line.

MAKE UP THE COVER
To make up the cover, cut out the pieces using the pattern as a guide.

1 Cut out the pieces
Pin the pattern pieces to the fabric, positioning the centre of the back and seat sections on a fold line where appropriate. Where there are narrow matching panels, for example down the wings of the chair or down the front of the arm, cut out both panels at the same time, through a double layer of fabric, so that the shape is reversed.

2 Make up piping
If you intend to insert piping in some of the seams, it is best to make up sufficient piping for your needs before starting to make up the cover. For most medium- to heavyweight piping cord, you will need to use 3.5cm wide bias-cut fabric. (For details of a quick method of cutting large quantities of bias binding, see overleaf.)

3 Pin the panels together
Pin the various pieces of the cover together. Insert piping into the seams as appropriate. Pin, tack, then stitch each seam in turn, checking the fit after tacking. Start by making up the arms and wings (if there are any), then fit them to the front, back and seat panels.

4 Add the skirt and fastenings
Finally, add the skirt (optional) and make the casing to draw the four flaps underneath the chair together to hold the cover in place. Turn under 1cm along each of the four long raw edges, then turn under a further 2cm. Pin, tack and stitch to make a casing. Measure each channel, and cut a length of tape to this length plus about 70cm. Thread tape through each casing in turn, starting from the opening corner.

◁ **A flash of colour**
Jagged stripes of brilliant colour have been used to create a loose cover for this upright wing chair. The straight skirt with box pleats at the corner emphasizes the vertical lines of the chair.

MAKING UP PIPING

Bias-cut strips can be very fiddly and awkward to join, so try this trick of joining the fabric *before* cutting out the strips.

1 *Find the true bias* ▷
Lay out a piece of fabric (about 1m by the width of the fabric). Check that it is a true rectangle (the top and bottom, AD and BC, are at right angles to the selvedges, AB and DC). Fold the corner A down to meet the bottom of the rectangle. The line BX is then the true bias. Press.

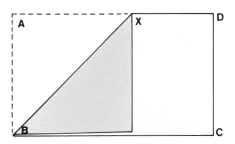

2 *Cut and re-join the fabric* ◁
Cut off the top triangle (ABX) and join selvedge (AB') to opposite selvedge (DC). Join with right sides facing, taking a 1.5cm flat seam. Press seam open. Measure and mark cutting lines 3.5cm apart parallel to the diagonal edges of fabric. Mark seam lines 1.5cm in from upper and lower edges (XX' and BB').

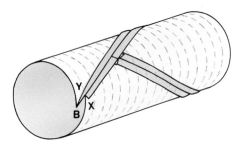

3 *Join the horizontal edges* ◁
Roll and twist the fabric into a cylinder, wrong side out, so that you can join the lower edge to the top edge. Stagger the diagonal markings (working from left to right, at the marked seam lines, each marked cutting line at the bottom will meet the previous one at the top). Make a flat seam; press open.

4 *Cut the bias strips*
Starting from point Y, cut out the bias strips in a continuous spiral to make one long strip, with a series of diagonal seams in it. Pin and stitch the cord into the bias strips so that you have a length of piping from which you can cut off just the amount you need, as you need it.

BRIGHT IDEA

THE ULTIMATE LOOSE COVER

If you don't feel you could manage a fully fitted loose cover, you could compromise with this loosely fitted cover, made up in panels.

Remove any seat and back cushions which are part of the piece. Measure from floor level, up the front of the seat, across the seat, over the back of the sofa and down to the floor at the back. Measure the width of the seat of the sofa. Add a

little extra to both measurements (about 20cm) to allow for a tuck in all round the seat. Make up a panel of fabric to these measurements, with a 2cm double hem all round.

For the arms, measure from the back of the sofa, right round to the centre front of the arm. Add 20cm to this measurement to give plenty of fullness at the front of the arm. Measure from the seat up the inside arm and over the arm to floor level.

Make up a panel to this measurement, taking 2cm double hems. With the main panel in place, arrange the side panels so that the back edge is tucked under the main panel. Gather fullness at front. When you are satisfied, decide on the best positions for the ties. Stitch cords in place. Add Velcro strips to the back edge of side panels, and stitch matching strips to back panel. Sew covers for seat cushions.

RE-UPHOLSTERING A DROP-IN CHAIR SEAT

Upholstery is a skilled task, but you can tackle small items such as a simple chair seat yourself.

Victorian and Georgian dining chairs often had simple upholstered drop-in seats. The seat lifts out, so they are easy to handle, and since re-upholstery involves little sewing, this type of seat is a good choice for beginners.

The actual shape and construction of these seats varies according to when and where they were made. There is usually a simple wooden frame, with webbing to support the stuffing, covered first with calico and then the top fabric. Some modern chairs have seats with a solid base and synthetic stuffing,

but these do not last as long as traditional webbed seats.

Because the construction varies, you should take the worn seat apart carefully so that you can check the techniques originally used. And if the seat was made from traditional materials (horsehair or a fibre mixture), it is worth re-using the stuffing since horsehair in particular is very difficult to obtain.

UPHOLSTERY FABRICS
Strong, firmly woven fabrics are the best choice for upholstery. Many manu-

facturers produce upholstery-weight fabrics in patterns to match curtain-weight fabrics, which make co-ordination easier. For a drop-in seat you also need various specialized materials.

Webbing is used to support the seat. It is stretched and nailed to the frame, with crosswise lengths woven in and out of the lengthwise strips. You can use black and white herringbone weave or strong brown jute webbing. It should be about 5cm wide.

Hessian is a loosely woven fabric which is laid over the webbing to provide a base to which the stuffing is attached.

Stuffing is available from upholstery specialists. Professionals agree that horsehair gives the best results, but it is expensive if you have to replace the existing stuffing. Try to recycle it if possible. Put it in a pillowcase, and wash it in soapy water and disinfectant, then spin it in a washing machine. Allow it to dry naturally, fluffing it out as much as possible. The best alternative is veg-

Smart seats
These Victorian dining chairs have been re-upholstered in an all-over trellis print. If you use a bolder pattern, place the motif carefully on the seats.

etable fibre stuffing such as coconut, though this is coarser. If you mix horsehair and coconut, use the horse-hair as the top layer. On top of the hair or fibre stuffing, you need layers of cotton felt wadding or synthetic wad-ding at least 2.5cm thick to make a pad large enough to cover the entire seat.

Twine holds the stuffing in place. You only need a small amount for a seat, plus a straight upholstery needle.

Calico is used to firmly cover the stuffing. You need a piece at least 10cm larger all round than the seat.

Tacks Webbing, hessian, calico and top covering fabric are all fixed by tacks: use 16mm upholstery tacks for the webbing and 13mm tacks for the rest.

CHECK YOUR NEEDS
Fabrics and materials
☐ Webbing (about 5cm wide)
☐ Hessian
☐ Stuffing (horsehair or vegetable fibre)
☐ Twine
☐ Calico
☐ Top fabric
Tools
☐ Upholstery tacks (16 and 13mm)
☐ Tack lifter
☐ Webbing stretcher
☐ Tack hammer
☐ Straight upholstery needle
☐ Curved upholstery needle (optional)

SPECIAL TOOLS
Upholsterer's tools are not large or expensive, so it is worth investing in a few items, particularly if you plan to tackle several projects. For this job, the following are useful:

Tack lifter A tack lifter is useful for stripping the old tacks from the frame.

Webbing stretcher Different people have different preferences for the shape and style of stretcher. One of the easiest to use is the type that is shaped like an hour glass, with rubber attached to one end (to protect the frame of the seat and prevent the stretcher slipping) and spikes at the other end to hold the webbing firmly.

Tack hammer Any fine hammer will do, but a magnetic tack hammer, which holds the tacks as you nail them, makes the job much easier.

Needle A fairly long, very sharp upholstery needle is essential. You may also find a curved upholstery needle useful. (Upholstery needles are often sold in mixed packs.)

PREPARING THE SEAT
The drop-in seat has to be stripped before the new cover can be attached. Make a careful note of the way the seat was assembled so that you can recon-struct it in the same way.

1 ***Remove the existing covering***
Spread a sheet out to collect the dust. Use the tack lifter to lift the tacks holding the existing cover, calico and stuffing in place. Put any horsehair into a pillowcase, wash it in soapy water and disinfectant, rinse and spread out to dry. Tease it out when it's dry and it will be as good as new.

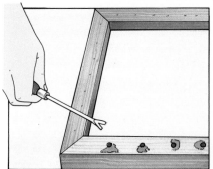

2 ***Remove the webbing △***
Remove the webbing and all the tacks which held it in place. If any tack heads break off as you remove them, knock the remaining nail into the frame to prevent it snagging the new fabric. It is not worth trying to save the webbing: if one strap has worn, the chances are that the rest will go pretty soon.

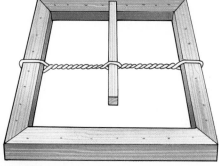

3 ***Check the frame △***
Check that the frame of the seat is firm and free of woodworm. Treat and then fill any tell-tale holes. If necessary, re-glue the joints, holding them with a tourniquet made by tying string round the sides of the frame and tightening it with a pencil or strip of wood as shown above.

ATTACHING THE WEBBING

When you are ready to nail the webbing in place, begin with the central, front to back strip, and then fill in with strips on either side. If the seat frame is old, try to position the webbing so that none of the strips have to be fixed at a point where the frame is riddled with holes. Do not cut the strips of webbing until they are stretched across the frame.

1 ***Nail one end of the webbing △***
Position one end of the first strip of webbing so that about 2.5cm hangs over the front of the frame. Nail in place with three tacks, as shown above left. Then fold the end back over the first three tacks and add a further two tacks in the spaces which remain, as shown above.

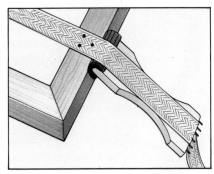

2 ***Stretch and nail the other end △***
Pull the webbing to the other side of frame and wedge the end of the stretcher against the frame. Ask a helper to hold the frame steady. Stretch the webbing by pushing the spiked end down, and fix with three tacks as before. This is the trickiest part: the webbing must be taut to give a firm base for the stuffing.

3 *Complete lengthwise webbing* ▷
Stretch and tack the other strips of webbing in place across the frame in the same way. Make sure that each of the strips is fully stretched.

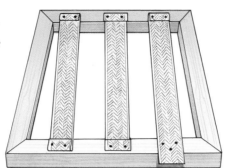

4 *Fix the crossways strips*
Fit the ends of the crossways strips in the same way. Fix one side of each strip in place, and then weave them under and over the lengthwise strips before stretching, trimming and finally tacking the other end in position. Again, make sure that the webbing is taut before tacking it in place.

STUFFING THE SEAT

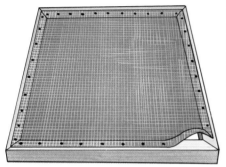

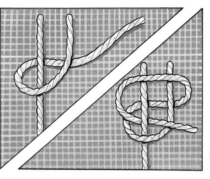

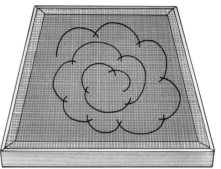

1 *Fit the hessian* △
Cut a piece of hessian 2.5cm larger all round than the frame of the seat. Turn over 3cm all round edge of hessian and lay it on top of the webbing. Tack in place, positioning a tack at each corner and about 5cm apart all round.

2 *Upholsterer's knot* △
An upholsterer's knot is a simple knot used to anchor the end of the twine. Thread twine on to the needle and take a stitch in the hessian. Use the short end to tie the knot, keeping the long end (and the needle) straight, as shown above.

3 *Make bridle ties* △
Bridle ties are simply loose back stitches. Start by making an upholsterer's knot, then take 8–10cm stitches over the hessian, leaving 10–15cm loops. Start at the centre and spiral outwards. Be careful not to pull the previous stitch too tight as you make the next one.

4 *Add the stuffing* ▷
Starting from the centre, pack the stuffing under the bridle ties. If you are using a mixture of fibres, start with the vegetable fibre and put the horsehair on top. Aim for a depth of about 6–8cm. Pat it in place to make sure there are no thin or low spots, and add extra stuffing where necessary.

5 *Position the wadding*
Cut the layers of wadding to the same shape and size as the frame and lay them over the stuffing. They should not overlap the edge of the frame, as this will prevent the frame fitting back into the chair. The layers of wadding should be about 2–3cm thick. The wadding gives a smooth finish, and prevents the stuffing from working its way out through the cover of the seat.

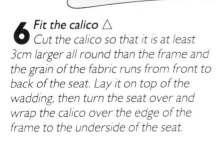

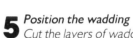
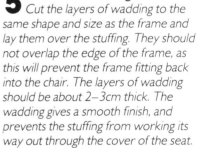

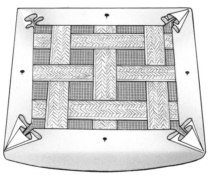

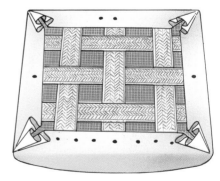

6 *Fit the calico* △
Cut the calico so that it is at least 3cm larger all round than the frame and the grain of the fabric runs from front to back of the seat. Lay it on top of the wadding, then turn the seat over and wrap the calico over the edge of the frame to the underside of the seat.

7 *Tack the calico in place* △
Check that the grain of the fabric is running straight, front to back, and stretch it tightly. Knock a temporary tack into the centre of each side of the underside of the seat. (Only drive the tack halfway in, so that you can remove and adjust it if necessary.)

8 *Fix the back and front edges* △
Starting with the front edge, tack the calico in place, spacing the tacks about 4cm apart. Start at the centre, then knock in a tack on either side and work out to the corners. Tighten the calico if necessary before repeating the process to fix the calico at the back.

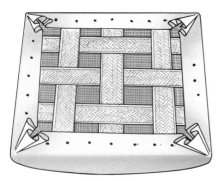
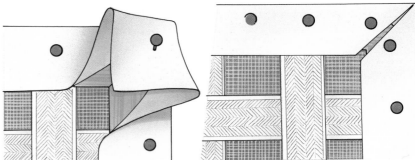

9 *The sides of the frame △*
Check that the wadding has not been pushed out at the sides. Trim away any excess if necessary. Then fix tacks down each side of the frame: work out from the centre, alternating from side to side, stretching the calico out to the corners as you go.

10 *Finish the corners △*
You should now have a tightly fitting calico cover, with a fair amount of surplus fabric at each corner. To neaten a corner, first open out the surplus fabric and turn the corner of the fabric in towards the centre of the seat. Tack in place temporarily so that the excess fabric is in a pleat on either side (above, left). Fold these pleats in towards the head of the tack to make a neatly mitred corner. Open out again and, using the fold lines as a guide, trim away excess fabric from inside the pleats. Re-fold the mitre and tack in place (above, right): repeat for each corner, checking that the calico on the top of the seat remains smooth.

11 *Attach the top fabric*
The covering fabric is nailed in place in exactly the same way as the calico. Make sure that the tacks do not coincide with the previous row of tacks. If you are using a fabric with a bold motif, check its position carefully before fixing it in place. If you are covering a set of chairs, position the same part of the pattern in the same place on each seat.

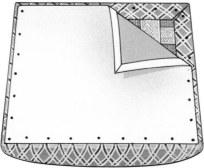

12 *Fitting the bottom cover ◁*
Finally, cut a piece of canvas or lining material 2.5cm larger all round than the frame of the seat. Turn under 3cm all round, mitring the corners and trimming excess fabric. Tack in place so that all raw edges are covered.

BRIGHT IDEA

NEEDLE WORK
A fine, Chippendale-style mahogany chair demands a smarter than average cover. This chair has been covered with Bargello needlepoint. Always work the stitching on a frame in order to hold the canvas square and prevent distortion. Limit the embroidery to the top of the seat cover so that there is no unnecessary bulk which might stop the seat from fitting back into the chair. Fit the embroidered panel over the calico cover in the usual way.

RE-CANING CHAIR SEATS AND BACKS

Repairing the seat or back of a damaged cane chair is fairly straightforward, but takes a little patience.

In Tudor times, British homes had few chairs, and those there were tended to be in heavy, dark oak. During the second half of the 17th century, French influences meant that lighter chairs, often with cane seats and backs, were introduced into this country. Cane continued to be used during the following centuries – many of Sheraton's chairs incorporated cane – and in the second half of the 19th century Thonet developed his famous cane-seated bentwood chair.

The use of cane continued throughout the Victorian era, and into the 20th century. However, modern cane on cheap furniture is often made up in sheets and stapled in place, rather than being meticulously woven through holes in the edge of the frame. It is not usually possible to replace sheet cane with traditionally woven cane, but if you do have a traditionally woven seat which has fallen into disrepair, you will save a great deal of money if you can re-cane it yourself. To check that the cane is traditionally woven, look under the chair: you will be able to see the ends of the cane woven though the holes round the frame of the seat.

The most widely used pattern, and the one which is described here, is the six-way pattern, which is made by weaving pairs of horizontal and vertical strands of cane, then diagonal strands.

BUYING THE CANE

You can buy cane for re-caning seats from specialist shops. It comes from the rattan plant, which grows in the tropics, mainly in the Far East. The part which is used for chair seats comes from the bark, and it has a glossy surface. It is cut into long strips of varying widths, and the inner part of the cane is cut into cylindrical strips and used for basket-making and for 'pegging', one of the procedures in caning chairs.

The strips of cane come in various widths. For seating you will normally need a combination of three widths: no2, which is about 2mm wide; no3, which is about 2.5mm wide; and no6, which is about 5.5mm wide, for the edging (or beading) to finish the edges in most cases. These sizes are recommended for most chairs, where the holes are about 13mm apart and about 4mm in diameter. Obviously, you may need to use larger or smaller cane if the size and spacing of the holes on the chair you intend to re-cane is different to this.

The cane is sold in bundles, by weight. A couple of 250gm bundles will be sufficient to do several chairs: some shops sell the cane in smaller quantities (enough for a single chair) which is a good way to buy it if you are a beginner.

You will also need some of the centre part of the cane, cut into short lengths and sharpened to a point, to hold the cane in place while you are working. Centre cane is also used to finish the holes once the cane has been worked (for further information see pages 91-92).

CANING TOOLS

The main items you will need are an old pair of scissors, a sharp craft knife or a pair of wire cutters (for clearing the old canework), a clearing tool (rather like a screwdriver or a bradawl with the end cut off), and a selection of implements (stilettos or bodkins, either curved or straight) to lift the cane during the later stages of caning. You can also use a shell bodkin – a long, curved implement with a groove down the inner face. As an alternative, use a pair of scissors to trim the end of the cane to a point, to make it easier to weave.

If you have golf tees around the house, or plastic, self-grip wallplugs, you may find these useful for pegging the cane to hold it in place while you are working on it.

Light work
The traditionally woven, six-way pattern is not as difficult as you might think. It is fairly strong, but not suitable for hefty dining guests – keep canework for side chairs which won't be subjected to heavy wear and tear.

PREPARATION

Before starting to cane a seat, first you must strip out all the existing cane. This is quite easy if the job was done properly in the first place: you simply cut the cane away from the chair, close to the edge of the frame. Keep the panel of cane you have cut away so you can check how it was done before, the size of cane used and which holes were used at each stage. Then cut away the beading round the edge, and use a special clearing tool to push the pegs and remaining cane out of the holes which have been exposed. If glue has been used, this may be tricky, and you will have to use a drill to clear the holes.

Once the seat is stripped, check whether any repairs are needed to the frame before starting the caning. For example, you may encounter one or more of the following problems and have to spend time treating wood-worm, re-finishing surfaces, repairing loose joints or levelling uneven legs.

Before you can start, you will also have to soak the new cane to make it pliable. This involves taking just a few lengths from the bundle and leaving them in a bowl of tepid water for a few minutes. You then take them out and wrap them in an old towel for 15 minutes, so they are pliable enough to work with. Just take one strand from the towel at a time, keeping the remainder damp. If the cane dries out too much as you work, dampen it by dipping your fingers in water and running them down the cane.

CHECK YOUR NEEDS
☐ Scissors, craft knife or wire cutters
☐ Clearing tool
☐ Hand-held drill and appropriate 4mm drill bit (if holes need drilling out)
☐ Materials for treating woodworm, re-finishing surface and dealing with loose joints
☐ No2 and no3 cane
☐ No6 cane for beading
☐ Centre cane to make pegs to finish the edges
☐ Centre cane, golf tees or wallplugs for holding cane in position while you work
☐ Sharp implement (stiletto or bodkin) for lifting the cane, or scissors to trim cane to a point
☐ Old towel

PREPARING THE FRAME

Before you can start, you have to cut away all the old canework. It's a good idea to keep the original piece of cane, even if it is badly damaged, to use as a guide, both to the size of cane used and the pattern, when you start to cane shaped pieces. If you have several chairs of the same pattern, only cut away one seat at a time, so that you can use the others as a guide at later stages of the process.

1 Cut away the main panel ◁
Use a sharp craft knife, a pair of old scissors or a pair of secateurs to cut away the old canework as close to the outer edges as possible. Don't discard the canework forming the seat or back of the chair at this stage. Note that the outer edge may be covered in beading cane, or held in place by a peg in each hole.

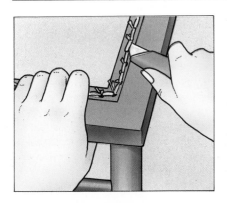

2 Remove the beading △
Beading cane is held in place by couching (strands of cane threaded over the beading cane). Use a craft knife to cut away this couching, taking care not to damage the chair frame.

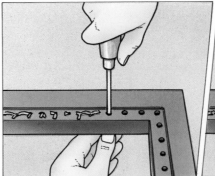

3 Knock out the remaining cane △
You will now be left with a few ends of cane sticking out of each hole. If there was no beading, you should have pegs in every hole; if there was beading, the pegs will be in alternate holes. Use a

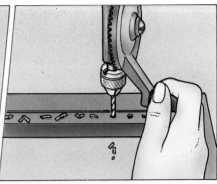

clearing tool to remove the remaining cane, tapping it with a hammer if necessary. If the cane does not come out easily, use a hand drill, with a drill bit the same diameter as the holes in the frame.

SIX-WAY CANING PATTERN

This pattern is the strongest, and most frequently used caning pattern. Here it is worked on a fairly square-framed seat – you can adapt the finish at the corners slightly to suit different shapes, using the original canework as a guide (see page 93). The first four stages of this pattern are usually worked in no2 cane, and the last two stages in no3 cane, which is very slightly wider. Soak the cane, a few strands at a time, putting it in a bowl of tepid water for a few minutes, then leaving it wrapped in a towel to keep it pliable.

1 Prepare the cane pegs
Cut lengths of centre cane into 5cm long pieces, and sharpen the ends with a craft knife (rather like sharpening a pencil – holding the point away from you). You'll need at least a dozen. You can use golf tees or wallplugs as pegs – they only hold the cane temporarily.

2 Test the cane
Take a strand of cane from the towel and test its pliability. At the same time check its strength, and check which way the grain runs – there are notches which catch if you use the cane the wrong way. Discard short pieces.

3 Find the centre holes
Count the number of holes across the back and front rails. Find the centre hole in each rail, and mark with a peg. Find the centre of a strand of cane.

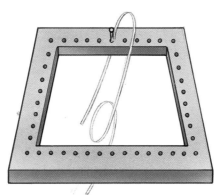

4 Start the first stage ◁
The first stage of the pattern is worked from back to front across the seat. Thread the cane down through the centre back hole, with the shiny side of the cane facing to the back, until the centre of the cane is in the hole. Peg it in place. You may find it easier to thread the cane, particularly at the fourth, fifth and sixth stages, if you trim the end of the cane to a point.

5 Bring cane to front rail
Bring the part of the cane on top of the chair to the centre hole of the front rail, remove the marker peg and thread it down through the hole, keeping the cane flat with the glossy side up. Make sure there are no twists in the cane. Pull it taut and replace the peg to hold it firmly in place while you work the next row.

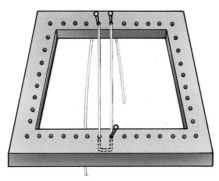

6 Thread up through adjacent hole ◁
Turn the cane under the chair, along the frame, then thread it up through the adjacent hole. (The dotted lines indicate where the cane lies.) Keeping it flat, taut and glossy side up, take the cane to the back of the chair, to the corresponding hole adjacent to the starting point. On future rows of caning, plan this 'underweaving' so you stagger where the lengths of cane show under the frame.

7 Continue the first stage
Thread the cane down through the appropriate hole in the back rail, pull taut, peg in place, then bring up through the adjacent hole. For each subsequent strand, move the pegs to hold the cane in the hole you have just threaded the cane into. This ensures that the work you have done is held taut. Work backwards and forwards across the chair until you reach the last but one hole in the back rail.

8 Dealing with the ends ▷
When you come towards the end of a strand of cane, peg it in place. Bring the new strand up through the adjacent hole, leaving a short tail (about 10cm) on the underside of the seat, and peg it in place. You can simply leave these ends, to be finished later, or tie them in to the loops of cane running under the frame of the chair as soon as you have worked the next couple of stages, to anchor them securely.

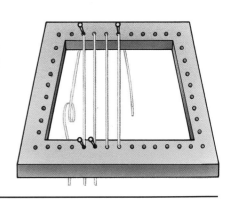

9 The sides of the chair ▷
When you have filled all the holes across the back of the chair except the corner one, peg the end firmly. The sides of the chair are usually angled, so you will find there are three or four extra holes in the front of the chair. Work separate lengths of cane, keeping them parallel to the strands you have already worked. Never carry the cane under the frame across more than one hole, as it will block the holes.

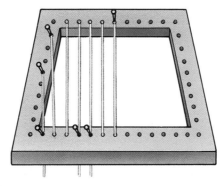

10 Finish the opposite side
Finish the first stage of vertical weaving by going back to the long end of cane in the centre back hole, bringing it up through the adjacent free hole, and completing the other half of the chair to match the first half.

11 The second stage ▷
Now take the cane from side to side, over the first stage. If the back of the seat is straight, start one hole down from the back corner on the right-hand rail. If it is curved, start one hole in along the back rail. Take the cane across the chair, glossy side up, taut and untwisted. When you come to a pegged hole, take it out, thread the cane through, then re-peg it.

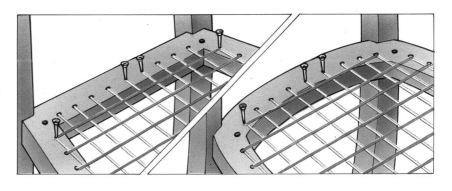

12 *The third stage* ▽
The third stage lies over the first stage, but slighty to the right. Start on one side rather than at the centre and work across. Use the same holes at the sides as for the first stage.

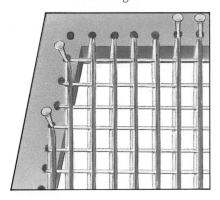

13 *Weaving the fourth stage* ▽
Now the real weaving begins. This stage involves threading strands parallel to and just above the second stage. However, these strands have to be woven under the first stage and over

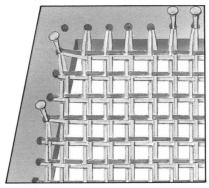

the third stage. Just thread the cane through the appropriate holes by hand, with one hand above the work and one below. Weave across four strands, then pull the cane taut before weaving under and over the next four strands.

14 *Using a shell bodkin*
You may find it easier to use a shell bodkin (a long, curved, scoop-shaped implement), to hold the third stage strands down while the fourth stage is threaded under the first.

15 *Keep it neat*
Work from side to side, keeping the cane glossy side up, taut and untwisted. Hold the work firmly in place with pegs wherever necessary.

16 *The fifth stage* ▽
This stage (and the sixth stage) is usually worked with wider, no3 cane. It is important that this stage is worked correctly to give a smooth, strong pattern. Start from the back, right-hand corner (there should not be any cane in this hole at this stage). Peg the end of

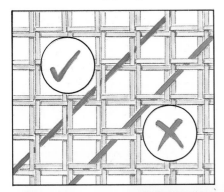

the cane in the corner. Weave the cane under the first pair of vertical strands, over the first pair of horizontals, and so on diagonally across the seat. The diagram below left shows the right and wrong way – the edge of the diagonals should nest between the verticals and horizontals.

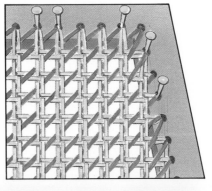

17 *Continue the diagonals*
Work across to the opposite rail (which may be the front rail or the left-hand side rail). Make sure the strand is straight and taut, and peg it in place. You now have to work back to the same corner you started from. If you are pegged to the front rail, move one hole to the left; if you are pegged to the side rail, move one hole forward. Then weave back across the chair, still weaving over the horizontal strands and under the vertical strands. Pull the cane taut and peg into the corner temporarily. Then bring the cane up through the next hole down the right-hand rail and continue as before. Go on until all the diagonals are woven from the back right to the front left.

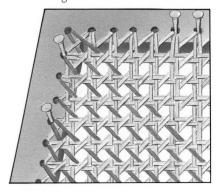

18 *Weave the sixth stage* △
The sixth stage is worked diagonally in the opposite direction, weaving over the vertical and under the horizontal strands to complete the pattern. You now have a six-way pattern, anchored with temporary pegs.

◁ *At your convenience*
Victorian commodes can be re-modelled (and re-caned) to fit around a modern WC. Note the different shapes of the seat and back, illustrating the versatility of six-way caning.

FINISHES FOR CANED SEATS

Once you've completed a simple chair seat, you have a choice of finishes. These pages also give hints on curved seats — and ideas for using ready-woven cane.

There is a choice of two finishes for caned seats: you can either replace the temporary anchors (the golf tees) with permanent pegs, made from lengths of cane, or use a combination of pegs and couching – a wider strip of cane, held in place over the holes with fine cane which is threaded through the holes.

Details of the most commonly used, six-way pattern are given on pages 87-90. Those instructions refer mainly to straight-sided chair seats. There may be particular problems with curved or circular chair seats, and on the following pages there are some examples to show how you can get an even finish at curved corners.

There are also various ideas for using ready-woven cane, which can be bought by the metre from specialist suppliers. It can be used to repair chairs and other furnishings much faster than by weaving it yourself, and there are several decorative effects you can achieve with a minimum of effort.

PERMANENT PEGGING

This involves cutting lengths of the centre cane so they are slightly shorter than the depth of the rail. You then hammer them into the holes, finishing by tapping them in with a clearing tool. You have to be careful not to upset the tension of the caning as you do this.

COUCHING

For a couched finish, you have to peg every alternate hole, and then lay a strip of fairly wide cane (beading) over the holes, and weave a finer cane through the unpegged holes to anchor the beading in place. You will inevitably still be able to see the peg in the hole you start from, but all the other pegs should be completely covered. This finish is best for straight-sided seats – it is more difficult to work on curves as you have to keep the cane flat as you ease it round corners.

COPING WITH CURVED SHAPES

The best rule of thumb for dealing with curved shapes is to keep the original cane, so that you can use it as a template. For particularly intricate shapes, it may even be worth photographing the original canework before removing it. The important thing is to get a smooth, even finish: with curved shapes, this often involves threading more than one cane into a single hole.

USING READY-WOVEN CANE

Ready-woven cane is a time-saving way of achieving the effect of hand-woven cane. It is often used in modern, mass-produced pieces of furniture. You can usually tell whether a chair seat has been made with sheets of cane by looking at the edges: where the cane meets the frame of the chair, there is a continuous 'filler' strip of centre cane, rather than pegged holes or couched cane. On the reverse side, there are no holes or ends visible.

The simplest way of fixing ready-woven cane is with a staple gun: the actual method depends on the situation in which it is being used.

The elegant touch
In this traditional setting, the cane chairs complement the fresh, light atmosphere of the room. The curved backs require a little more skill than the squarer shapes of the seat: it is advisable to keep the panels as a guide to renewing the canework.

INSTANT AGEING
Old canework has an attractive patina, so that it is a deep golden shade rather than the cold buff colour of new cane. Whether you have done the caning yourself or used ready-woven cane, you can give it a distressed look by applying a woodstain (not water-based). It is worth testing the effect on a scrap piece first, to ensure you get a good colour. It is usually easier to get an even effect with a cloth rather than a brush.

◁ *Are you sitting comfortably?*
The slight 'give' of canework makes it particularly comfortable for the seat and back of a rocking chair. With a curved seat panel, thread the first and third stages (horizontally) then weave both the second and fourth stages.

PERMANENTLY PEGGED FINISH
This is a more traditional finish for canework than couching, and is a better choice for curved frames.

1 *Prepare the pegs*
Cut lengths of centre cane slightly shorter than the depth of the chair frame. Check they fit the holes snugly: you may have to pare them down to fit.

CHECK YOUR NEEDS
For finishing canework:
☐ Centre cane for permanent pegs
☐ No6 and no2 cane for couching
☐ Light hammer
☐ Clearing tool
☐ Sharp scissors

For working with ready-woven cane
☐ Sheets of ready-woven cane
☐ Sharp scissors and craft knife
☐ Staple gun
☐ Pencil, ruler, measuring tape
☐ Saw and mitre box
☐ Hammer, panel pins, wood glue and beading

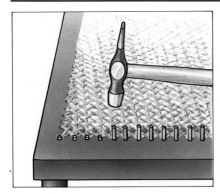

2 *Knock in the pegs △*
Use a lightweight hammer to tap the pegs into the holes, removing the temporary pegs as you work.

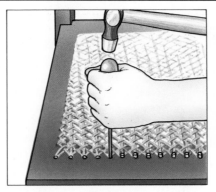

3 *Tap the pegs home △*
Use the clearing tool like a nail punch, to tap the pegs slightly below the surface of the chair frame.

4 *Finish the underside △*
Trim away any odd lengths of cane which are hanging down below the chair frame.

COUCHED FINISH

A couched finish can help to disguise any irregularities in the weave, and produces a neater edge.

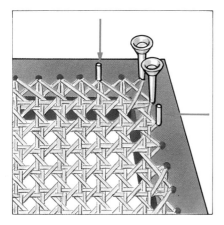

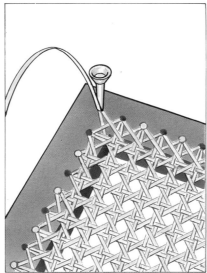

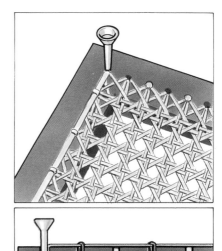

1 Peg the holes △
Tap pegs into every other hole, leaving each corner hole and the holes on either side of it free. If there are temporary pegs holding cane in holes which will not be pegged, take the ends of the cane round to adjacent holes and thread them up before pegging. Hold these ends in place as you knock the pegs into the holes to prevent them being pushed back down through the hole, then trim the ends close to the pegs.

2 Starting the beading △
Starting from the back, left-hand corner, bring one strand of no6 cane up through the hole and one strand of no2 cane down through the hole. Peg in place temporarily. The no6 cane runs down the edge of the canework, over the holes and you only need four short lengths, each slightly longer than the side of the chair it has to finish. You need longer pieces of the no2 cane, as this forms the couching, weaving under and over the beading.

3 Position.the beading △
Lay the no6 cane over the row of holes on the left-hand rail, glossy side up, keeping it flat and taut. Bring the working end of the no2 cane up through the hole next to the corner hole, over the no6 cane and back down through the same hole again, taking care not to twist it. Then bring the cane up through the next unpegged hole. Continue down to the next corner.

4 Turning the corner ▷
Take the second length of no6 beading cane and thread it up through the corner hole. Thread the end of the first piece down through the same hole. Anchor the beading canes with a permanent peg, positioning it so that the second piece of beading cane covers the peg when you fold it down to start the next rail. If you need to start a new length of no2 cane, thread the ends up through the corner hole to anchor them as in Step 1. Continue round to the hole you started from, starting a new length of beading cane at each corner.

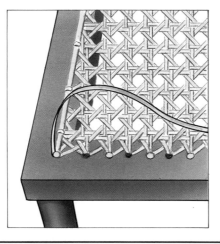

5 Finishing off
Finally thread the couching cane up through the last hole and the beading cane down through the same hole. Knock a peg into the hole, taking care not to let the finer canes slip out.

6 Trim the ends
On the underside of the seat, trim off the ends of cane close to the frame of the chair, as neatly as possible. Any ends you find which are not permanently pegged should be tied in: dampen the end, then thread it round the couching running under the frame.

CURVED FRAMES

The only problem with curved frames is that you will find you have to weave several strands into some of the holes on the corners. It is impossible to give detailed instructions for every shape, so here are two examples showing how to cope with a typical curved corner, and a completely circular seat.

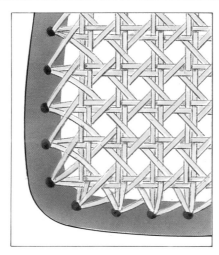

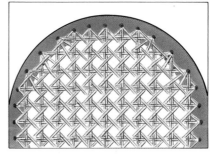

1 Corner detail ▷
On chairs with curved corners, two or more holes will have to take two diagonal canes (rather than just the corner hole taking two diagonals, with squarer shapes).

2 Circular shapes △
The same principle applies to completely circular chairs: three or four holes will have to accommodate two diagonal canes.

USING READY-WOVEN CANE

Ready-woven cane is available from specialist shops by the metre (or yard) – it is about 60cm (24") wide. It has to be soaked before use: this makes it more pliable, helping to prevent it from splitting and breaking. Ready-woven cane can be used in a variety of situations – for example to cover a headboard, or to add interest to a flush door. In most situations it is necessary to cover the edges of the panels with beading for a neat finish. Normally, the surface behind the cane panel and the beading are painted to match the surrounding surface. By using contrasting colours, however, you can achieve some interesting effects: black paint behind natural cane panels can look very dramatic, while soft green or grey gives a more subtle effect.

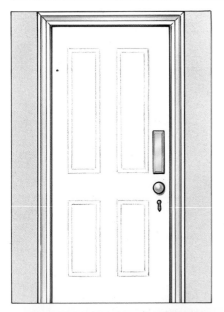

1 *Mark the area to be covered* ◁
Mark the area you wish to cover carefully: decide what type of beading you are going to use, and mark the positions for both the inner and outer edges of the beading, using a pencil.

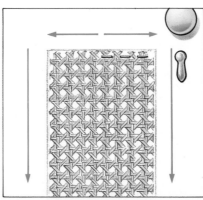

2 *Soak the cane*
The cane usually comes in a roll, just over 60cm wide. Soak it in a trough or bath long enough to take the full width of the roll. Leave it in warm water for about 10mins.

3 *Cut the panel*
Cut out a panel of cane, about 1cm larger all round than the finished area it is to cover. Follow the pattern, even if it doesn't appear to be quite straight.

4 *Fix the cane* ◁
Using a staple gun, fix the cane in place. Start at the centre top of the panel, work out to either side, then work down each side and across the lower edge. Position the staples so they will be covered by the beading.

5 *Trim the cane*
Use a sharp craft knife to trim away the ends of the cane, just inside the outer marked line.

6 *Fit the beading* ▽
Measure the beading accurately and mitre the corners. Fix in place using wood glue and panel pins.

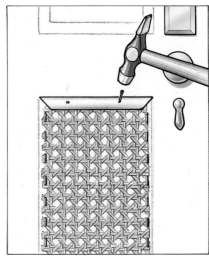

◁ *Covered with cane*
A sheet of ready-woven cane, stretched over a wooden frame, has been fitted into a housing to cover a radiator. The light structure of the canework and the slatted top of the housing allow air and heat to circulate.

INDEX

PHOTOGRAPHIC CREDITS
Front cover Romo Fabrics, 1 EWA/Spike Powell, 2-3 IPC Magazines/Robert Harding Syndication, 4-5 IPC Magazines/Robert Harding Syndication, 6 IPC Magazines/Robert Harding Syndication, 7 Arthur Sanderson Ltd, 8 Syndication International, 9(t) Textra, 9(b) Sunway Blinds, 10(t) National Magazine Co/Good Housekeeping, 10(b) EWA, 11 EWA/Michael Dunne, 12(t) Sunway Blinds, 12(b) Syndication International, 17(tr) Net Curtain Advisory Bureau, 17(b) Swish, 18(t) Harrison Drape, 18(b) Textra, 19(t) Osborne and Little, 19(bl) Osborne and Little, 19(br) Net Curtain Advisory Bureau, 20(tl) Net Curtain Advisory Bureau, 20(tr) Chas Hammond, 20 IPC Magazines/Robert Harding Syndication, 21 Textra, 22 Net Curtain Advisory Bureau, 24 Arthur Sanderson Ltd, 25 Sue Stowell, 26(tl) Dulux, 26(tr) Textra, 26(b) Nicholas Holt, 27(t) Harrison Drape, 27(bl) Textra, 27(br) Swish, 28(t) Chas Hammond, 28(b) Kingfisher, 29 Harrison Drape, 30(t) Osborne and Little, 30-31 Perrings, 31(t) EWA/Michael Dunne, 32(tl) Rufflette, 32(tr) Kingfisher, 33(tr) Harrison Drape, 33(b) Net Curtain Advisory Bureau, 34(tl) Swish, 34(tr) Bill McLaughlin, 34(b) Sunway Blinds, 35 Syndication International/Jerry Tubby, 38 Kingfisher, 39 EWA/Michael Dunne, 42 Bill McLaughlin, 43 Dylon, 46 Jahres Zeiten Verlag, 47 Di Lewis/Eaglemoss, 51(t) EWA/David Cripps, 51(b) Crown Paints, 52(tl) Jacqueline Bateman, 52(tr) Dulux, 52(b) Crown Paints, 53(l) Richard Paul, 53(r) Guy Bouchet, 54(tl) EWA/Jerry Tubby, 54(tr) Liberty, 54(bl) EWA/Michael Dunne, 55 Designers Guild, 56(t) Charles Hammond, 56(b) Bill McLaughlin, 57(t) PWA International, 57(b) EWA/Spike Powell, 58 EWA, 59 FADS, 62 Pallu and Lake, 63 Jan Baldwin/Eaglemoss, 66 Jan Baldwin/Eaglemoss, 67 Skopos Designs, 70 Richard Paul, 71 Jerry Tubby/Eaglemoss, 74 Jerry Tubby/Eaglemoss, 75 Graham Seager/Eaglemoss, 76 Graham Seager/Eaglemoss, 77 Graham Seager/Eaglemoss, 78 Graham Seager/Eaglemoss, 79 Jan Baldwin/Eaglemoss, 81 Collier Campbell, 83 Jan Baldwin/Eaglemoss, 86 Tom Belshaw, 87 EWA/Michael Dunne, 90 David Hicks, 91 Syndication International, 92 Richard Paul, 94 Bill McLaughlin.

KEY: EWA - Elizabeth Whiting Associates